PAPER

TEAR • FOLD • RIP • CREASE • CUT

black dog
publishing

CONTENTS

Richard Sweeney, *Floral Corsage for Boudicca*, 2006, paper, adhesive, photo: Richard Sweeney

FOREWORD

Paper presents us with the opportunity to create seemingly limitless variations of form, structure and composition. It is the tactile quality of paper that is so appealing—there are very few materials capable of presenting such a diversity of form-making through manipulation solely by hand. This physical connection with material is perhaps the most important aspect in the development of work in paper.

The prevalence of hand-craft in the creative world today is perhaps surprising given the dominance of digital techniques. I believe it is the sheer physicality —the ability to mould, shape and play with physical 'stuff'—that makes paper manipulation a far more immediate and intuitive means to create objects, visuals and works of art.

Paper is not only a sculptural material in its own right, but a tool that can be used to bring ideas into a physical reality before they evaporate. I hope this book will inspire the reader to see paper with a new-found respect, and to embrace the creative potential of this most humble material.

Richard Sweeney 2009

PAPER

The birth of paper originates from a need to write, illustrate and document; it is the medium on which marks are made. But when creative attention is turned to the material itself, the medium becomes the object and the true personality of paper emerges.

Inherent in the material is a delicate fragility, and this is reflected in the manipulations that can be applied to it, from the softness of the fold to the sharpness of the cut. In Japan this idea is perhaps best understood, where the philosophy of the art of Japanese paper folding is closely tied with the art of papermaking itself. The process of making Washi, a traditional Japanese paper closely allied with origami, is a revered art and the various types of Washi reflect different personalities based on the choice of fibres used.

Literally translated as 'Japanese paper', Washi is a unique paper made from the long inner fibres of three different plants, all native to Japan—Kozo, Mitsumata and Gampi. Each fibre is chosen for what it represents and the resultant Washi reflects the characteristics of the fibre. Kozo is considered a masculine ingredient; thick and strong, it delivers a tough, resilient paper. Mitsumata on the other hand is considered feminine, and as such graceful and modest. It delivers a delicate and soft paper, and because the plant takes longer to grow, it is more expensive than the more widely used Kozo. The age of Gampi fibre meanwhile bestows on it a reputation for nobility, dignity and richness. With a seductive sheen, Gampi is often used in very fine, tissue-like sheets, and does not bleed when written on. More generally, Washi is known for its warmth, its body and its strength.

While Washi represents a gold standard in paper, at the other end of the spectrum, cheap, grey, mass-produced pulps made from discarded materials such as old cotton and linen rags have defined the everyday appearance of paper right up until the discovery of bleaching in the nineteenth century. The existence of such a wide range of grades varying in value, quality, texture and finish is a direct result of the way in which it has developed throughout history from a valuable commodity into an everyday necessity.

Paper was first created in order to replace the use of inadequate materials such as bamboo and silk as writing surfaces. Cai Lun, officer in charge of instruments and weaponry during the Han Dynasty in China, is believed to have first formed paper in AD 105 using a formula no longer known but probably consisting of materials such as bark, hemp or silk. Cai Lun's creation was met with such gratitude that not only did he receive an aristocratic title and significant wealth, but he was also subject to reverence in the practice of Chinese ancestral worship. The Chinese historian Fei Zhu recorded in the Song Dynasty several hundred years later that a temple had been erected in Chengdu in honour of Cai Lun, where hundreds involved in the papermaking industry flocked to pay their respects. The invention of paper not only improved communication, but had a great impact on the spread of literature, and consequently on national literacy. As the potential of paper became apparent, so it expanded into mass use. Meanwhile, despite this steady increase in production and availability, its association with royalty meant that high quality papers with a potential beyond that of pure writing material continued to be developed.

The Definition

True paper is made from macerated fibres thinly intertwined to produce sheets. This is in contrast to the early alternatives, which included papyrus, made from sliced sections of a plant known as *Cyperus Papyrus*, and rice paper, which was cut from the pith of rice paper trees. Parchment and vellum, meanwhile, are made from the skins of animals, and while not actual papers, they were seen as preferable in Europe for many centuries as paper was seen as an Eastern development and consequently treated with undue suspicion.

The gap between the East and the West meant that the secrets of 'true' paper manufacture was confined initially to the East. The technology of making paper moved from China to Japan and then to Korea in AD 610. It also found its way via caravan from China to Samarkand, a city whose influence derived from its central position on the Silk Road between China and the West. Yet the secret to its creation remained closely guarded until centuries later, when China lost a battle in Turkistan in AD 751 and Turkistan found skilled paper makers amongst their prisoners. Samarkand, as it happened, was perfectly suited to developing paper: rich in the resources necessary to make it—specifically hemp, flax and pure water—it provided
a launchpad for its development in the West.

Paper In Europe

Europe remained surprisingly resistant to paper for centuries. The Church in Western Europe initially outlawed the 'pagan art' of paper use in favour of continued use of animal parchment in the belief that this was the only acceptable medium on which sacred texts could be carried. By the fifteenth century, however, the reputation of paper had changed to such an extent that the King of England at the time, Henry VII, even paid a personal visit to the first British paper mill. This was a far cry from five hundred years earlier, when the famous Domesday Book had to be written on parchment. Yet paper did exist in Europe around that time—the oldest recorded paper document in Western Europe was a deed of King Roger of Sicily, dated 1102, and the first European paper mill is thought to have opened at Xátiva in Spain shortly after, in 1120.

Aside from general hostility towards paper's origins, there was less immediate need in Britain to replace vellum and parchment due to a large and steady supply of sheepskin, from which it could be made. Yet the value of parchment began to rise in inverse proportion to that of paper during the fifteenth century, a direct result of the increasingly widespread availability of paper mills. In 1588, paper finally found a home in Britain when John Spilman opened a mill near Dartford in Kent. A German entrepreneur, he brought the knowledge of native papermaking with him and made a success of his mill through the patronage of the monarchy, much like the inventor of paper, Cai Lun, many centuries earlier. It was this mill that attracted the most influential figure in England, the King himself; paper had finally become an essential medium throughout the world.

Paper Manufacture

Throughout the history of papermaking, the art has required a long and often expensive apprenticeship. The secrecy that surrounded the formulae and manufacturing methods, and played its part in suppressing the spread of its manufacture globally, was an integral part of the industry.

A common method of manufacture would see the fibres pulped in water and then mixed in a deep vat. Up until around the thirteenth century, the fibres of mass-produced pulps were almost entirely derived from linen and cotton rags. A mesh or mould was dipped into the vat to pick up the pulp, and would then be transferred to a wooden frame with a raised edge, known as a deckle, which then held it in place. As the pulp was still in a liquid form at this stage, the excess would flow out of the frame around the sides, creating the soft, irregular edge familiar on handmade papers today. It is from this that the term 'deckle-edged' has come into use. When the layer of pulp was ready, it would be transferred to a piece of felt, with another piece of felt placed on top and pressed down to remove any excess liquid. The remaining paper 'sheet' would then be hung to dry. Early Chinese papers were constructed on bamboo moulds, which allowed for a degree of flexibility. In Europe, however, the discovery of paper came hand in hand with a new wire mould, which better suited the materials that were used at the time.

The quality of paper depended on the material from which it was made. As a result, it was not only for aesthetic reasons that the whiter papers carried more value—the material from which they were made was of more direct value too, with cheap grades made from 'found' fibres carrying a dull grey, yellow, or uneven colouration. This discoloured paper dominated in the Medieval period. The finer papers, on the other hand, were produced from cotton and linen that was woven by hand specifically for the purpose.

Today, the whiteness of paper is achieved through bleaching, but this practice dates only from the nineteenth century. Previously, British paper remained stubbornly grey, while France tried to add a blue dye to counter the somewhat unpleasant colouration. Inclusions—specks of dirt within the paper—have always been a problem in papermaking, and their absence has always been an easy way of identifying a very fine paper grade. Today, however, inclusions can be a welcome addition to speciality papers. People using recycled papers in printing often prefer to see a sheet with a peppering of marks to show clearly that the paper has been produced from this process. Equally, it marks an absence of chemical whitening, which can have a negative environmental impact, meaning that an untreated paper has come to have a degree of ecological caché. Speciality papers also make a feature of their inclusions: paper maker GF Smith have a paper named 'Bier' made from old beer bottle labels, where flecks of the unusual recycled material liberally pepper the page.

The Art of Paper

The long history of paper manufacture reveals it to be as much an artform as a factory exercise, and the quality and character of the paper itself reflects this artistry. Throughout history, artists have been strong in their pronouncement of preferred paper surfaces, but in Japan and China in particular the paper itself has been seen as a part of the art. It is from this aesthetic appreciation of paper that paper folding has developed in Japan, and paper cutting in China, to be traditions closely tied to the character of the countries themselves.

In the West, paper has tended to remain primarily a medium on which to write or illustrate, rather than an object in itself. Recently, however, the potential for the manufacture and manipulation of the material as an integral part of a piece of art or design has increasingly been explored. Artists featured in this volume not only fold and cut paper to create artforms in their own right, but many implicate the process of paper manufacture in the work itself. Riki Moss, whose grand installation *Studio Glow* (p. 104) emits a warm, delicate light through heavy, twisted folds, is constructed from pulps that she has treated herself—manilla hemp abaca paper overbeaten for several hours in a Hollander beater, with embedded materials that allow her structures to support themselves despite their weight. Jewellery designer Nel Linssen, on the other hand, subjects her chosen paper to plasticisation in order to enhance the sharpness of the folding structures and open them up to a wide colour spectrum (p. 162). In the area of furniture design, Jens Praet has taken recycled paper in a direction that makes the material from which his furniture is made its defining feature, creating solid structures from shredded paper documents mixed and compacted with resin.

Such approaches to paper manipulation in art and design continue the rich legacy inherent in its manufacture, whereby altering and experimenting with process and ingredient have achieved exceptional results; the potential for those working with paper today to carry on this tradition and innovate is as vast as it is diverse.

FOLD·CREASE

by Hatori Koshiro

The origins of origami, the art of paper folding, are unknown. While it is commonly thought that origami originated in China around two thousand years ago, directly following the invention of paper, there is no actual evidence to support this. The history of the former Han dynasty in China, from which paper is thought to have originated, shows no trace of origami. The Chinese character for paper, *zhi*, originally stood for writing material made of silk; the origin of the Japanese word for paper, *kami*, is said to be birch tree, *kaba*, or strips of wood or bamboo, *kan*. Both were also writing materials, suggesting that paper was primarily used for writing, not folding.

Another school of thought suggests that origami originated from Japan in the Heian period (AD 7794—1185). This belief derives from a Japanese legend that tells of Abe-no Seimei, who was said to have made a paper bird and brought it to life, and another story about Fujiwara-no Kiyosuke, who sent his ex-lover a model frog. However, there is no evidence to suggest that the bird and frog were folded from paper.

In Japan today, paper called *tatogami* or *tato* is used to wrap and store kimono; it dates back to the Heian period and can be seen as an early example of paper folding. However, it is by no means an example of origami as an art form, since it involves only square folds.

In the practice of the Japanese religion Shinto, paper strips known as *shide* or *heisoku*, and paper dolls known as *hitogata*, have existed for many centuries. However, while they existed in ancient Japan, they were never made of paper, and are not necessarily folded even now. Despite the reverence with which the art of paper folding is practised, there appears to be no relationship between Japanese religion and the origin of origami. Although the Japanese words for paper and gods have the same spelling, 'kami', in ancient Japanese, they differed in their pronunciation, implying a difference of meaning.

The word 'origami' originates from the Heian period in Japan, yet it initially referred to a form of writing: an 'origami' is a landscape piece of paper folded in half latitudinally. Letters or lists are usually written on it. In fact, paper folding was not known as origami in Japan until the Showa period. It was known previously as *orisue* or *orikata* in the Edo period, and *orimono* from the end of Edo period to the early Showa period.

Japanese Classic Origami

The oldest unequivocal document of origami is a short poem composed by Ihara Saikaku in 1680 which reads: "The butterflies in Rosei's dream would be origami". Here, Saikaku referred to an origami model called *ocho mecho* (male and female butterflies) as *orisue*. It is still used to wrap sake bottles at Japanese wedding ceremonies today.

Origami was included in the traditions of the samurai class, which were passed down by the Houses of Ogasawara, Ise, Imagawa and others. Folds such as *ocho mecho* and *noshi* are examples of this ceremonial origami. Many folding patterns exist for many purposes. According to Ise Sadatake's *Tsutsumi-no Ki* (Book of Wrapping) of 1764, such origami originated in the Muromachi period.

More familiar origami models such as *orizuru* (crane) and *yakko-san* have been depicted in *ukiyoe*, or patterns for kimono, since the eighteenth century. The book *Ramma Zushiki* of 1734 shows pictures of *boat*, *sanbo* (box), and a modular origami shape called *tamatebako*, besides *orizuru* and *komoso*. The origin of these models is unknown.

Some differentiate such recreational origami from the ceremonial equivalent, but in the Edo period this distinction does not seem to be apparent. In Saikaku's *Koshoku Ichidai Otoko* (The Life of a Lustful Man) of 1682, the protagonist Yonosuke made *orisue* of *hiyoku-no tori*, which is supposed to be a similar form to that of *orizuru*. Nor did Adachi Kazuyuki separate ceremonial and recreational origami when he recorded many origami models in his book *Kayaragusa* around 1845.

Akisato Rito published *Sembazuru Orikata* in 1797. *Sembazuru* literally means 'one thousand cranes', but at that time it referred to dozens of connected *orizuru* folded from one sheet of paper. It is sometimes said to be the oldest book dedicated specifically to origami in the world, but in fact it is only the oldest of its kind, *Tsutsumi-no Ki* of 1764 being older.

Based on these sources and others such as the anonymously authored *Orikata-dehon Chushingura* of 1800, an understanding of the characteristics of Japanese classic origami can be teased out. Classic origami involved many folds, including judgement folds and multiple cuts. The design was very much dependent on the quality of Japanese handmade paper, Washi. To make a coloured pattern, multiple sheets of different coloured papers would be used, as is common today, and sometimes even paint. The use of paint and cutting is anathema to the origami purist today, but it is a misconception to believe that in eliminating them they are getting closer to the art of origami as it was originally manifested.

European Classic Origami

Contrary to popular opinion, origami is not a 'Japanese' art. A picture in the 1490 edition of the book *Tractatus de Sphaera Mundi* by Johannes de Sacrobosco (John of Holywood), which was reprinted over 60 times during the seventeenth century, appears to be the same as that of *boat* in the book *Ramma Zushiki*. If it really is an origami boat, it is unlikely to have descended from Japan, since Japanese origami at that time would have existed, if at all, in purely ceremonial form.

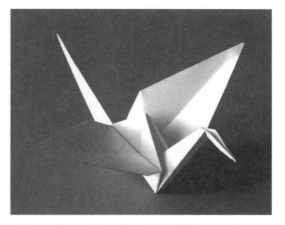

Unknown, *Orizuru/Peace Crane*, single folded paper sheet

John Webster referred to a 'paper prison' in his play *The Duchess of Malfi*, which premiered around 1614 and was published in 1623. It probably relates to an origami model known as water bomb today. It does not appear in any Japanese sources of the Edo period.

Some unequivocal references to the origami of the nineteenth century can be found all across Europe. Among others, the collections of the German National Museum and Museum of Saxon Folk Art have origami horses and riders, which are thought to have been folded around the first half of the nineteenth century.

In the mid-nineteenth century, Friedrich Fröbel established the world's first kindergarten. His educational system included the use of toys, referred to as 'gifts', and plays, described as 'occupations'. One of the occupations was undoubtedly origami. Fröbel's gifts and occupations were separated into three categories: forms of life, forms of beauty, and forms of knowledge. Ordinary origami was categorised as one of the forms of life. In the origami of forms of beauty, symmetric patterns are developed from an initial blintz fold (a common method of folding all corners of a square into the centre). Elementary geometry is taught in the origami of forms of knowledge.

Only a few models of nineteenth century European origami can be found in contemporary Japanese sources. Even now, very few Japanese folders know *pajarita* ('little bird') though every Spanish folder knows it. On the other hand, the *orizuru* model was not known in Europe at that time even though it was typical of Japanese classic origami.

The models of European classic origami have a character of their own and distinguish themselves in the base of their structures. Japanese folds tended to rely on creases of 22.5 degrees, whereas European folds tended to be at 45 degrees. European origami generally focused only on square or rectangular paper, and usually avoided judgement folds and cuts. European and Japanese classic origami were so different that they seem almost to have developed independently.

The origin of European origami is also unknown, but it is thought that it may relate to the baptismal certificate of the sixteenth and seventeenth centuries. At that time, baptismal certificates were folded into double blintz or the Japanese model known as *menko* or 'thread holder'. It is thought that this ceremonial origami may date back to the fifteenth century.

Hatori Koshiro, *Pli Selon Pli No. 2*, Paper with pleated folds

Traditional Origami

Despite the common belief that origami was born in Japan and migrated, both Japan and Europe had a developed notion of origami when Japan closed its borders in 1639. The origami of the two regions were fairly independent until the Meiji Restoration in the nineteenth century, and the following exchange between Japan and Europe then led to a fusion of Eastern and Western origami.

Japan imported the Fröbelian kindergarten movement, which contained European classic origami, when they rebuilt their educational system in the style of the European one. Similarly, Western kindergartens adopted Japanese classic origami. Thus Japanese and European classic origami were mixed, and the subsequent repertoire of origami that evolved in Japan has been passed down and forms the core of what is now defined as traditional origami. Japan also started to produce origami paper, a square of Western paper coloured on one side, because of the needs of kindergarten to teach Fröbelian origami. Since the Meiji period, new models have been added to traditional origami, many of which are suitable to fold with origami paper, while at the same time many models suitable to fold with Washi were dismissed.

In traditional origami, modelling techniques were passed down from generation to generation, and their shapes and titles changed frequently. Children, as well as adults, often tended to make variations or even improvise new models. This creativity, inherent in traditional origami, is one of the reasons that Fröbel included origami in his 'occupations', but in today's origami education, pupils are taught simply to follow the sequence as it exists already. As a consequence, teachers, under the misguided belief that learning traditional origami involves mere imitation, have come to exclude it from their education.

The models of traditional origami travel a long distance in a short time, sometimes beyond borders, as people move. Japanese *orizuru* migrated to Europe and became 'flapping bird' in the first years of the Meiji period. Then Miguel de Unamuno, who was active from the end of nineteenth century to the early twentieth, made many models based on flapping bird.

Traditional origami has been born and brought up in the cultural exchange between East and West. It is not a Japanese original culture but intrinsically a hybrid of Japan and Europe. Although most popular in Japan, its popularity was inherited in Europe, the Americas, China, and beyond from the nineteenth century and into the early twentieth.

Modern Origami

In traditional origami, the folding sequences and titles are passed down as something anonymous, not as something made up by a specific person. Modern origami, which started in the twentieth century, is based on an

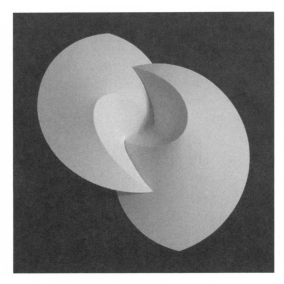

Matthew Shlian, *State*, 2000, Folded paper

entirely different paradigm. The folding sequences of modern origami
are regarded as 'models' which are 'designed' by 'origami creators'.

The father of modern origami is Uchiyama Koko, as he patented his origami
models. Today many people believe that origami models should be copyrighted,
the idea that particular persons have intellectual property in folding sequences
being a typical characteristic of modern origami. In modern origami, the
creativity is attributed to the designers, and the appreciation to the folders.
Modern origami shows an appreciation of models that have not only good
final shapes but also good sequences. In addition, it places importance on
the reproducibility of the model; that is, according to proponents of modern
origami, folders should aim to reproduce the shape as it was originally
conceived by the designer.

Diagrams representing the entire folding sequence of a model are important
in modern origami, as they represent the model itself. Similar representations
of model folding exist in Japanese classic origami, but they do not describe the

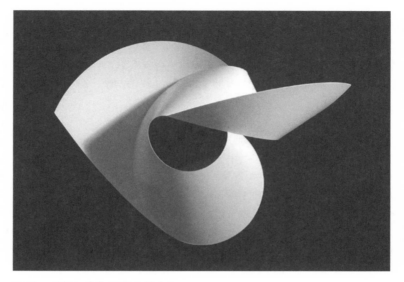

Matthew Shlian, *Shell*, 2000, Folded paper

entire sequence, leaving aspects of the folding process up to the imagination of the individual folders themselves. In modern origami, some emphasise the aspect of origami as the puzzle of reproducing the shapes of objects under a certain rule, the most common definition of that rule being to fold one sheet of square paper without cutting or gluing.

Behind the rule, there is the implicit premise that origami models should be folded with origami paper. Practitioners make a point of the ease of origami —that is, to do origami, nothing is needed but origami paper. Thus, a model made of more than one sheet of paper is regarded as good when it is made of sheets of the same size and can be assembled without glue.

In the 1950s and 1960s, an international origami circle was established by creators and folders such as Yoshizawa Akira, Takahama Toshie, Honda Isao, Robert Harbin, Gershon Legman, Lillian Oppenheimer, Samuel Randlett and Vicente Solórzano-Sagredo. They advanced the popularisation of origami through their community, publishing the origami models of designers from

Japan, Europe and the Americas in Japanese and English. They also founded national and local organisations. 'Origami' became a universal word because of Oppenheimer's work, while Yoshizawa's notation of diagrams was adopted by Harbin and Randlett, and became the international standard.

Mathematical Origami

Different origami models are often assigned to the first stage of a certain model's sequence. Consequently, many models have some halfway shapes in common. Such halfway shapes are known as bases, and are illustrated in diagrams as a flat sheet with lines to represent initial folds. Among the first surveys of these bases were those of Uchiyama Koko in the 1930s and that of Vicente Solórzano-Sagredo in the 1940s.

The new models in modern origami depend heavily on a few established bases. 'Bird base', which is the halfway shape of *orizuru*, is used to create not only birds but also animals or flowers. New bases are rarely invented, although sometimes variations are made, such as 'folding bird base' from a triangle or using a combination of both 'bird base' and 'frog base'.

Richard Sweeney, *Floral Corsage* (maquettes), 2007, paper, adhesive, For Boudicca collection 'An Artificial Paradise', photo: Richard Sweeney

When a base is folded and unfolded, a crease pattern is formed. Geometrical studies of crease patterns have been made since the 1980s, and has paved the way for the invention of new bases. As a result the meaning of the base has completely changed. In the new method, if a creator was to design a new model, say *pegasus*, she or he would not choose one from existing bases but make a new *pegasus* base. This is known as 'mathematical origami'.

Maekawa Jun and Peter Engel independently started such origami. Both of them noticed that the crease patterns of established bases consisted of particular triangles and rectangles. They divided crease patterns into these 'atoms', and rearranged them to make new patterns. In other words, they designed new models before they folded them, rather than arriving at a design through the process of folding itself.

The advanced theory has been developed by Meguro Toshiyuki, Kawahata Fumiaki, Robert Lang, and others. In this theory, a base is regarded as a set of independent areas distinguished by the length and arrangement of the areas. They devised algorithms that would generate the crease pattern of a base from an arbitrary length and arrangement of areas. Lang's *TreeMaker* is a computer program which supports origami design based on his algorithm. Some other design methods do not depend on existing bases. Among them, the box-pleat is widely applied, a method pioneered by Max Hulme and Neal Elias in the 1970s.

Combining these design methods, complex models can be made with only one sheet of square paper and without scissors. Thus, the notion of origami as a 'puzzle' with a solution is increasingly emphasised in mathematical origami. That is, mathematical folders compete in designing realistic or complex models under the rule of one sheet of square paper with no cuts. In addition, crease patterns are regarded as an important part of the model alongside the final shape and the sequence.

Artistic Origami

The word 'origami' consists of *oru* (to fold) and *kami* (paper). However, those who emphasise the aspect of origami as a puzzle tend to overlook this. In 'mathematical' origami, paper is reduced to mere geometrical shapes such as the square or the rectangle, and the folds to mere geometrical manipulations.

Reflecting on Japanese classical origami, it cannot be said that the essence of origami is purely in its geometry. Many models of the Edo period, for example, are based on the characteristics of Washi. For example, catfish, water lily, or *sembazuru* cannot be folded with Western paper without tearing, whereas they can easily be folded with Washi. Moreover, the point of ceremonial origami is not to make the shapes but to express the folder's sincerity.

Since the 1950s, Yoshizawa Akira has searched into the expression of folding paper, and demonstrated that origami has the potential to be a fine art. He has

Unknown, *Origami Ball*, 2008, paper, no adhesive

enhanced the expressive potential of origami and has had a great influence on today's artistic origami. His works not only represent the appearance of the objects, but also show emotional expression. They are not lifelike; they live their own lives.

In the 1960s, Uchiyama Koko created *kamon-ori* or 'flower pattern folding', which produces abstract patterns based on geometrical expansion of tato. At the time, abstract origami itself was not new; in fact, it dates back to the Fröbelian origami of 'forms of beauty'. But Uchiyama shaped unique art works by folding multi-layered Washi that he had dyed himself.

Folders of artistic origami bring out the potential expressiveness of the paper. Therefore the choice of paper is important. In addition, they often work on the paper and improve its expressiveness. Uchiyama's *kamon-ori* is an excellent example, as is Yoshizawa, who innovated wet-folding by dampening paper before folding. He also tried expression using cut edges of paper. Michael LaFosse, meanwhile, makes the paper himself.

Works of artistic origami are folded paper, and so the creativity is attributed to both the designers and folders, and the appreciation to the viewers. The sequences or the crease patterns themselves are not the object of appreciation. In addition, there is no reproducibility in artistic origami, because the same sequence would produce different works with different types of paper or different folders.

Today, Western folders are more active in artistic origami. Among the exponents of abstract origami are Jean-Claude Correia, Paul Jackson, and Vincent Floderer, and those of representative origami include Eric Joisel, Michael LaFosse, and Giang Dinh. These artists represent a new generation of origami folders who are taking the art of folding into fresh and distinct new territory.

CUT·RIP·TEAR

The cut, much like the fold, has been used as a means of artistic expression almost since the invention of paper itself. The earliest surviving example is a circular cut that dates from sixth-century China, but it was almost a thousand years later that this predominantly Eastern art form reached Europe and began to spread throughout the rest of the world.

The concept of the paper cut is simple in principle but it is in the process of the cut itself that the character of the art lies. A steady hand and an unhesitating, fluid movement will deliver the results distinctive of traditional cutting, but break this process, and the paper cut will fail. It is precisely this delicacy, and the potential for the cut to be destroyed with one small error of judgement, that inspires the character of the art. The distinctive quality of paper cutting was also defined by its capacity for hand-crafted duplication. This early form of 'mass production', achieved by layering up sheets of paper then cutting through them simultaneously, sealed its fate as a decorative art with considerable commercial value.

Today, the paper cut still exists in its traditional form, particularly in China and Switzerland, but elsewhere it has taken more challenging and divergent paths. Contemporary practitioners such as the Japanese artist Kako Ueda and American paper sculptor Chris Natrop have taken the appearance of the traditional detailed cut and spread them over vast areas to create large-scale installations (pp. 82 and 93), while other artists have reinterpreted the concept of duplication, such as Noriko Ambe, who has generated layered cuts in order to create the appearance of geographic topographies (p. 34). Major artists

Pan Baoqi, *Dragon and Phoenix*, 1970, Collection of the Guangzhou Museum of Art

have also incorporated layered cuts to create effects with conceptual resonance—Anish Kapoor's *Wound* consists of pages of a book 'wounded' with a knife; the effect is a fissure through the heart of the volume. Works such as these seem only a distant echo of early paper cutting, but the practical principles remain the same.

Traditional Paper Cutting

The style of the traditional paper cut as it is practised is immediately recognisable. A familiar structure involves an intricate lace-like lattice-work mirrored down a central crease to create a detailed, symmetrical pattern, which is then reproduced in several different forms in regularly numbered series. Chinese cuts are produced either by knife or by scissor, each delivering their own distinctive effect. Using scissors, several pieces of paper are layered up, fastened together, and then cut through. The knife-cutting procedure

Johann Jakob Hauswirth, *Alpaufzüg*, 1856, hand-cut paper

involves placing multiple sheets of paper on a soft base, traditionally made out of tallow and ashes. A free-cutting process ensues, often with the base-mounted paper held vertically.

Early Chinese paper cuts originally tended to be either purely decorative or designed as gifts that promised various states of wellbeing such as health and prosperity. Often cut from red paper, the 'language' of the Chinese cut was kept minimal, with designs focusing either on a single or a few Chinese characters, often reflecting the signs of the zodiac. When used decoratively, these paper cuts would often be displayed on doors and windows, giving rise to their alternative name 'Window Flower'. In China today, paper cuts remain primarily decorative symbols of good luck and prosperity, often reflected in the content of the cut itself—a standard depiction, for example, documents the attainment of happiness through noble actions.

Unknown, *Hibiscus and Butterfly*, Foshan paper cut, undated, Collection of the Guangzhou Museum of Art

When paper first came into existence during the Han dynasty, it was a valuable commodity available only in royal circles. Early expressions of paper cutting were highly developed but exposure beyond this sphere was limited. It was not until the practice became associated with festivals that its popularity became more widespread. References to paper cutting exist throughout the dynasties, but by the end of the Qing dynasty (1644–1911), despite technical advances in cutting, it was increasingly overshadowed by new and fresher developments in art. From then on, while it continued to be practised in rural areas, its status as a national pastime diminished across the region.

Today, it lives on in rural areas, where it remains a traditionally female activity. Curiously, the mastery of the art was considered a good signifier of suitability for marriage. In contrast, professional paper cutters in China are predominantly male, operating in a professional working environment with guaranteed incomes.

Paper cutting as an industry is perhaps best illustrated by the town of Foshan in the Guangdong province of China. Positioned on the point of intersecting waterways, Foshan enjoyed the benefits of considerable cultural and economic trade. As a result, Foshan cuts developed a very distinctive and highly-developed style that was characterised by the use of multiple different coloured papers and the use of copper-cutting templates rather than free-flowing, artistic cuts. During much of the Qing dynasty there were around 30 shops specialising in cut paper in Foshan, and the art flourished. Foshan cuts were not designed for royalty; rather they had a more mainstream appeal, and were used frequently in festivals, depicting popular imagery such as fish, birds, dragons and even opera singers. The process of carving through a template meant that Foshan paper cuts were open to production in bulk. As the late Qing dynasty gave way to the Republican period, changes in customs, aesthetics and industry altered the status of Foshan cuts and their popularity and mass use went into a steady decline. Increased governmental control also had an impact, leading to the production of overwhelmingly ideological paper cuts during the 1960s and 1970s under its direction. In 1966, the traditional practice of depicting 'door gods' was considered an unacceptable product of feudalism and was banned. By the 1980s, the political focus of paper cuts became suddenly unpopular, further cementing the end of the Foshan paper cut, driven as it was by market value. Now, the art form exists only marginally in the area, and remains in decline. It is a reflection of the status of paper cutting across the country in which it was first born.

Paper Cutting Around the World

Although Chinese cutting is the most developed and well-known of paper cuts, other countries have their own traditional variations. In Japan, *kirigami*, from *kiri* (to cut) and *gami* (paper), is a variant of origami in which cutting is also employed. The classic cut snowflake effect is distinctive of *kirigami*, although the term can also be ascribed more specifically to origami pieces where cutting has been used—an approach not favoured by origami purists.

The rare Indian variant of paper cutting, *sanjih*, is one of the more interesting variants of the art form, rich in ritualistic value and drawing on the aesthetic beauty inherent in the art. Bright coloured cuts are amassed in large quantities to create dazzling visual displays with religious significance. During religious festivals, vast amounts of cut paper are placed on the floor and the colours are filled in in-situ to create what is known as *rangoli*. *Sanjih*, with its probable origins in the words *sancha* (the mould from which the stencil is cut), and *sanjh* (the coming of dusk, when *rangoli* is traditionally unveiled in temples), is a rare process that has run alongside rangoli-making, for centuries a focal part in the ritualistic worship of the gods. The craftsmen of Vrindavan in the Uttar Pradesh region are amongst the few who continue to practise *sanjih*, their work depicting episodes in the life of Krishna. In temples in northern India dedicated to Lord Vishnu, stencils cut from banana leaves and paper are used to produce *rangoli* that embellished the courtyard of the temples' inner sanctum. During the religious festival known as the Vraja Yatra, *sanjihs* were unveiled during evening prayers and then disposed of the next day. The colours that fill in the *sanjih* are made from an assortment of fresh flowers, coloured stones, metal foil, pieces of mirror, and coloured powder.

Kako Ueda, *Eros and Thanatos*, 2007, hand-cut black paper (site-specific wall relief), 198 x 173 cm, Courtesy George Adams Gallery

More functional paper cuts have also had a presence as a Jewish art form since the middle ages. In 1345, Rabbi Shem-Tov ben Yitzhak ben Ardutiel claimed in his treatise *The War of the Pen against the Scissors* that he had written his manuscripts by cutting letters into paper, having discovered that his ink had become frozen. By around the seventeenth century, paper cutting had taken on the role it had adopted elsewhere in the world, becoming popular for religious artifacts such as *mizrachs* (decorative plaques designed to indicate the direction of prayer in Jewish households) and *shavuot* decorations. Today, it has been revived in Israel, and continues to be used for *mizrachs* and Jewish marriage contracts.

In Switzerland, where a paper-cutting tradition almost equal to that of China developed, paper cuts were also adapted to legal documents. This had a decorative appearance but a more functional application—to protect documents against forgery, much in the way that banknotes have come to contain watermarks and embedded metal strips. Given this function, the legal cuts were distinct to the cutter.

In contrast there is little of legal, symbolic, or religious value in most contemporary paper cutting, which tends to be far more freeform than the traditional variants of the practice elsewhere. There is a variety and a freshness to contemporary paper cutting that is pushing it in new directions beyond the confines of its flat, traditional appearance.

The Contemporary Cut

In modern artistic practice with paper, the cut is not necessarily fixed so tightly to the styles emerging from the Chinese paper-cutting tradition, most of which, from a cursory glance, bear some resemblance to each other due to the rules to which they adhere. Gone are the symmetrical patterns depicting folk and religious imagery clipped neatly according to intricate and precise patterns. In its place, deliberate folds and cuts occur alongside looser creases and tears, which in turn carry with them a freer, more spontaneous personality. Mathematical shapes formed through pleating, cutting and folding in the contemporary works of Richard Sweeney take their lead from the forms of mathematical modular origami and take them into fresh artistic territory (p. 45), while Siobhan Liddell's spiralling cuts are sharp and geometric, curling out of the page with an almost emotional anxiety. The way in which these contemporary takes on paper cutting and folding take on emotional resonance alongside their visual beauty associates them with the traditional Japanese appreciation of the 'personality' of the medium, and its ability to convey that personality in different forms through the actions carried out upon it, from the tear to the crease.

In Japan, contemporary paper cutting has crossed the boundary from form to function: Tokujin Yoshioka has taken pleating, folding and cutting into the area of furnishing, and his Honey Pop Chair folds out from layered cuts in tissue paper (p. 176). The aesthetic beauty of the fold and the cut is aligned not with conceptual significance but structural practicality, the apparently flimsy flat paper construction of the Honey Pop Chair able to concertina outwards into an object that bears a human weight, and the imprint of he or she who sits there.

Another interesting vein of contemporary cutting has developed which focuses on the most ubiquitous of paper objects: the book. Books have a structural simplicity and a deliberate focus—to transmit information. Contemporary interest however has led many artists to turn the attention to the medium itself. Artist Robert The takes inspiration from modular origami in his book cuts; his work *Desert Rose* is a progressive modular construction built out of a series of up to 60 King James Bibles from which the centres have been cut out (p. 122). Ellen Bell, meanwhile, cuts up the book in order to encourage a reinterpretation of the words printed on the paper (p. 128), while Georgia Russell dices her books and places them in specimen jars, so that they resemble primordial lifeforms immortalised in glass (p. 174). Ueda and Natrop articulate their indebtedness to the tradition more directly, deliberately taking traditional cutting techniques and updating them for a modern audience. On the cutting-edge of the art form, traditional style and contemporary ideas come together and breathe new life into the paper cut.

PAPER

ART

NORIKO AMBE

Through her complex organic structures built from cut and layered paper, Noriko Ambe attempts to map what she describes as the "mysterious land between physical and emotional geography". She sees the essence of nature in its detail, and aligns humankind with nature in her work. Her first paper series, 'Linear-Actions Projects by Drawing and Cutting', 1999, resembled both the annual rings of a tree and a topographical map, although the forms themselves actually described the traces of human activity.

Ambe avoids cutting mechanical or perfect lines in her work, preferring subtle, natural distortions that convey the nuances of human emotions, habits, or biorhythms. For this reason, each of her structures is meticulously crafted by hand. When drawing or cutting lines, she observes the power of the changing and growing shape and tries to harness it. This dynamic form, as it develops, becomes an entity, and another geography, in itself.

Born in Saitama, Japan, in 1967, Noriko Ambe received a BFA in oil painting from Musashino Art University, Tokyo, in 1990. She lives and works in New York and Tokyo, and began crafting work from paper in 1999. Her piece *Flat Globe*, featured here, is in the permanent collection of the Whitney Museum of American Art. *A Piece of Flat Globe Vol. 6* was exhibited at the 'Second Nature' Exhibition, directed by Tokujin Yoshioka, at 21_21 Design Sight, Tokyo (see p. 176).

A Piece of Flat Globe Vol.5 (detail)
2008
Cut on Yupo (synthetic paper), glue
17 x 15 x 17 cm

ABOVE & OPPOSITE
A Piece of Flat Globe Vol.4
2008
Cut on Yupo (synthetic paper), glue
15 x 22 x 15 cm

FOLLOWING PAGES
A Piece of Flat Globe Vol.6
2008
Cut on Yupo (synthetic paper), glue
13 x 17 x 15 cm

'Second Nature' exhibition, directed by Tokujin Yoshioka
at 21_21 DESIGN SIGHT, Tokyo
Courtesy of the artist and SCAI THE BATHHOUSE, Tokyo

Photos: Masaya Yoshimura

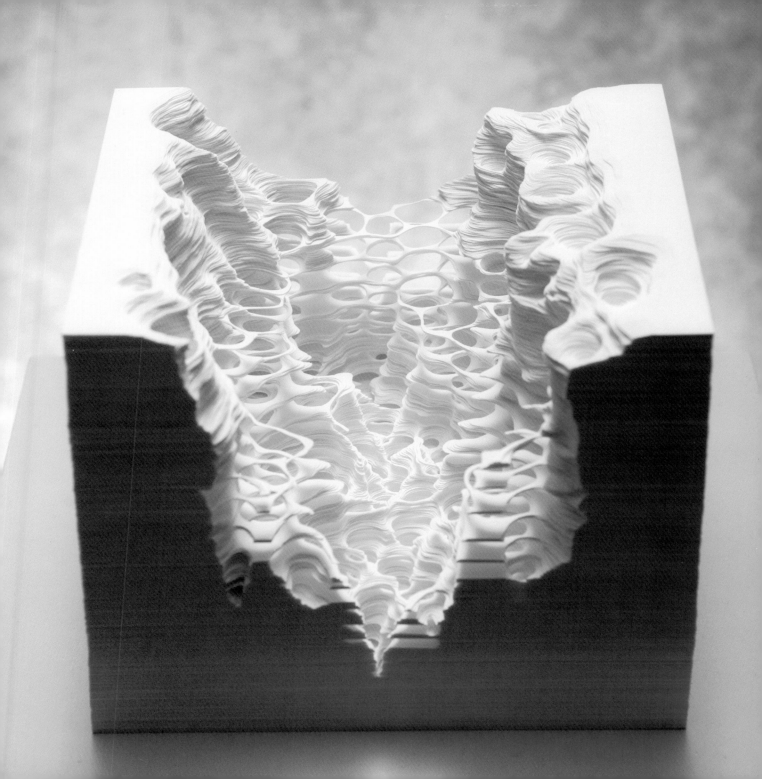

SIOBHAN LIDDELL

The emphasis of Siobhan Liddell's work is on subtlety.
Her paper structures push out of flat surfaces and
engage with their space through the interaction of
ambient light on their delicately reflective textures.
The result is a body of work that, through its complex
yet unassuming nature, holds a quiet, abstract power.

A profound simplicity is palpable in Liddell's
works and it comes from a meditative approach to
material and process, a quality which is also reflected
in the way in which form and meaning evolves in the
works throughout the duration of their construction.
Asunder and *Abandon* capture this intangible quality
while reflecting forms that are at once organic,
hypnotic and suffused with the character of paper.

Siobhan Liddell was born 1965 in Worksop, UK.
She now lives and works in New York City.

OPPOSITE
Asunder
2008
Acrylic on paper on canvas
127 x 178 cm

OVERLEAF
Abandon
2007
Paper on canvas
127 x 198 cm

Courtesy the artist and CRG Gallery,
New York

RICHARD SWEENEY

The paper sculpture of Richard Sweeney exploits the process of hands-on manipulation in order to 'feel' the properties of paper and tease out its behaviours. His works combine repetitive geometry, curved lines and modularity, building on developments in technology that have allowed geometric design to be mapped out through computer programming.

Richard Sweeney first explored sculpture through initial hand-drawn layouts which he translated to Autocad and then recreated as three-dimensional paper models in an experimental process that had no pre-determined outcome. Realising the potential of paper as a sculptural medium in its own right, he began to look beyond these early experiments in folded construction, developing them further in a manner that still embraced the initial spirit of experimentation but also incorporated elements of art, craft and design. The results are elegant, enigmatic paper sculptures which often break down the divisions between function and aesthetic. Sweeney's works vary from pleats and modular folds to freeform structural installations, all pushing the boundaries of folded paper architecture.

Icosahedron
2006
Paper, adhesive
Diameter 28 cm
Photo: Richard Sweeney

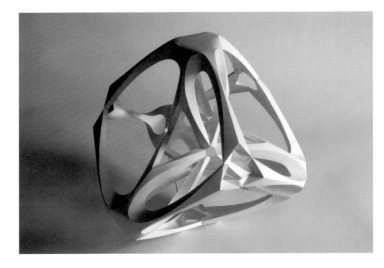

Tetrahedron
2006
Paper, adhesive
Diameter 46 cm
Photo: Richard Sweeney

SURFACE

Surface is a sliceform—a form comprising several intersecting, cross-halved sections—created for the Festival of Arts event 'Cartasia', held in Lucca, Italy, in September 2007. Computer modeling using 3D Studio Max and the construction of paper maquettes were used to achieve a piece that had a good balance between form and structural strength.

Achieving an effective scale was an important part of the design process; it had to be small enough to be produced on-site within the allotted time-scale of four days, yet large enough to make a presence in the town square. Once the design was finalised and approved, each slice was drawn out using computer programme Autocad, then printed at full scale to create a template for the transference of the design onto cardboard. The process of transference was achieved through a traditional method of using pin-pricks to mark out the new shape. Once cut by hand, each slice was waterproofed by covering all exposed edges with paper tape, then painting with a PVA-based medium. Wooden slats were placed beneath the piece to raise it, thus protecting it from the pooling of water on the ground.

Surface
2007
Cardboard waterproofed with PVA
Piazza Cittadella, Lucca, Italy
400 x 200 x 200 cm
Photo: Richard Sweeney 2008

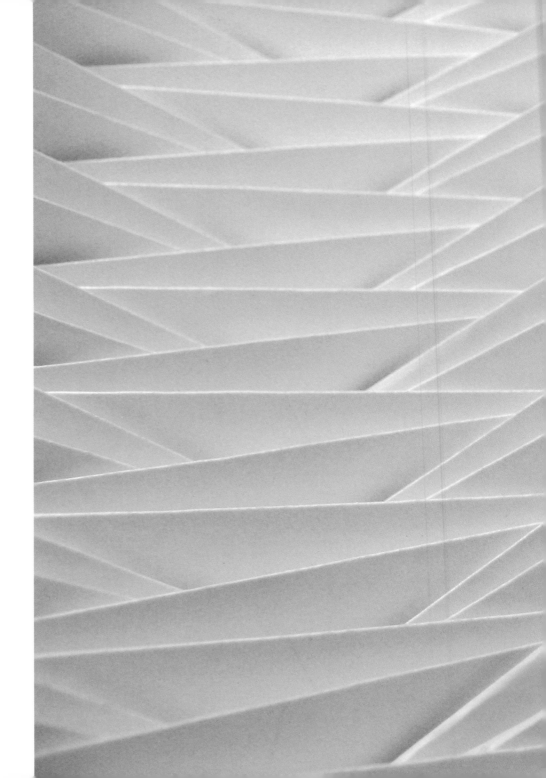

Richard Sweeney
Pleated Curve
2006
Hand-pleated paper
Photo: Richard Sweeney

MÖBIUS

Möbius is a series of sculptural works in paper commissioned by Selfridges for display in the flagship store windows on Orchard Street, London.

Of *Möbius*, Richard has said: "I had an idea of the kinds of form I wanted to produce—flowing, twisted and asymmetric, akin to diagrams of complex protein structures or twisted geometric figures such as the Möbius strip." An interesting aspect of this work is that the form of the pleated paper is dictated by the manner in which it is suspended. Without the selective effect of gravity maintaining the volume of the piece, it would simply collapse and revert to a flat form.

To create it, small models were suspended in a mock-up of the window space as a means of testing the behaviour of the pleated sheet when suspended. A total of 36 sheets were hand-scored and pleated over three days. In the window space, the sheets were glued end-to-end to create continuous lengths. The tension in the sheets caused by the angled pleat allowed them to be suspended in a natural manner—in other words, they were not forced into any particular configuration, but arranged according to the behaviour of the sheet.

Möbius
2008
Paper, adhesive, monofilament nylon
Selfridges flagship store, London
Photo: Richard Sweeney

MIA PEARLMAN

Mia Pearlman makes site-specific cut paper installations; ephemeral drawings that inhabit space in both two and three dimensions. Her works are a meditation on chance, control and the ephemeral nature of reality. They are a reaction to the overwhelming knowledge that is now available of every aspect of our world, from the smallest nanoparticles to the incomprehensible vastness of the universe, and the way in which this hyper-awareness has the potential to be simultaneously awe-inspiring and soul-crushing. As such, they evoke environmental chaos, physical instability, and infinite destructive forces that exist beyond human control.

To create them, complex line drawings are drawn on large rolls of paper in India ink; then selected areas are cut out to create a new drawing made from positive and negative space on the reverse. Once they are pinned into a sculptural form, these forms create a drawing in space, and a further 'shadow drawing' on the environment surrounding the three-dimensional structure.

Since receiving her BFA from Cornell University in 1996, Mia Pearlman has exhibited internationally in numerous galleries, non-profit spaces and museums, including Smack Mellon (Brooklyn, NY), the Centre for Recent Drawing (London), and Roebling Hall (New York). In 2009 her solo show 'Maelstrom' opened at the Montgomery Museum of Art in Montgomery, Alabama. Pearlman lives and works in Brooklyn, NY.

Eye
2008
Paper, India ink, tacks, paper clips
Centre for Recent Drawing, London

EYE

Eye is a cloud vortex swirling around the sky itself. Seemingly suspended between the visible world inside the gallery and an invisible world beyond the physical space, it appears to exist in a dimension that transcends interior and exterior. *Eye* was installed at the Centre for Recent Drawing in 2008.

EDDY

Eddy is a conceptual drawing on many levels: in the initial stage the shapes were drawn in India ink. Then selected areas were cut out to create a new drawing, made from positive and negative space, on the reverse. Once they are pinned into a sculptural form, a drawing suspended in space is created, its shadows producing a wholly new drawing on and around the three-dimensional drawing. *Eddy* was installed at

'I Wonder if you Know What it Means', curated by Christine Zehmer, at the Sears-Peyton Gallery in 2008.

PAUL HAYES

The site-specific installations of Paul Hayes consist
of vast swarms of crumpled or folded pieces of paper
suspended on strands of wire, evoking birds in flight,
schools of fish and other fluid patterns found in
nature. Hayes generates a sense of sweeping movement
in an attempt to capture the nature of currents,
motion and time; his works immerse the viewer
in a world where the man-made, processed quality
of paper is returned to its organic roots in nature.
"I enjoy working in large spaces, and transforming
an otherwise unremarkable environment into one that
triggers the imagination," Hayes says of his approach
to his work. "I sometimes think of it as composing a
drawing that can be physically entered."

Born in Massachusetts in 1977, Hayes received
a BFA from Rhode Island School of Design in 1999,
and has been living and working in San Francisco,
California, since 2001.

ABOVE
School
2007
Suspended paper
Installation at SOTA

OPPOSITE
Cultivated Momentum
2008
Suspended paper
Installation at Johansson Projects

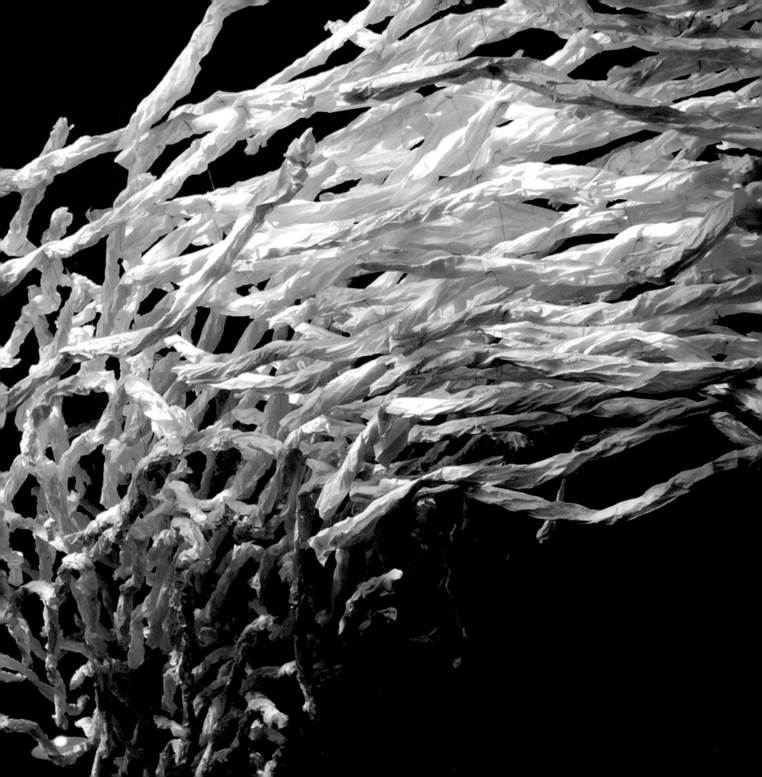

MATT SHLIAN

Matt Shlian's works are realised through curiosity—when a system of folding is initiated, the outcome is unknown, led as it is by the qualities of the material. It is, in his own words, a process of exploration as well as invention. Matthew Shlian's beautiful folds have more to them than their aesthetics alone. His application of engineering skills to create kinetic sculpture have lead to collaborations with scientists at the University of Michigan, where he has worked on a nanoscale, translating paper structures to micro origami.

Feeding into this is a fascination with computer technology, not in terms of its intended function, but rather in terms of its ability to mistranslate information. This potential for creating the unknown through fragmentation and misreading lends an added creative energy to his sculptural experiments.

His investigations at Michigan have extended to visualizing cellular division and solar cell development. "Researchers see paper engineering as a metaphor for scientific principals," he explains. "I see their inquiry as a basis for artistic inspiration."

Untitled
2008
46 x 30 x 30 cm

MATT SHLIAN   61

YUKO NISHIMURA

Yuko Nishimura developed a natural connection
with the art of folding through its daily expression
in Japanese life—from folding kimono to folding
wrapping goods in shops. Her inspiration comes from
the simplicity with which paper art can be created
from just one sheet, and without ever being touched
by a tool.

Aiming to produce work that will both show
respect for the history of paper-folding and appeal
to future generations, Nishimura does not limit the
language of her practice to a specific area of origami,
pursuing instead all possibilities of folding paper. As a
result, her works range from structured pleats to subtle
spiralling patterns that both pay homage to origami
traditions yet diverge into new territories. Yuko
describes her motivation as the desire to "express the
Japanese soul through form," and to breathe fresh life
into an artistic practice that continues to be "passed
down from generation to generation".

OPPOSITE
Tsurunaru-Katachi
2004
40 x 60 x 60 cm

OVERLEAF
Organic
2006
100 x 100 cm

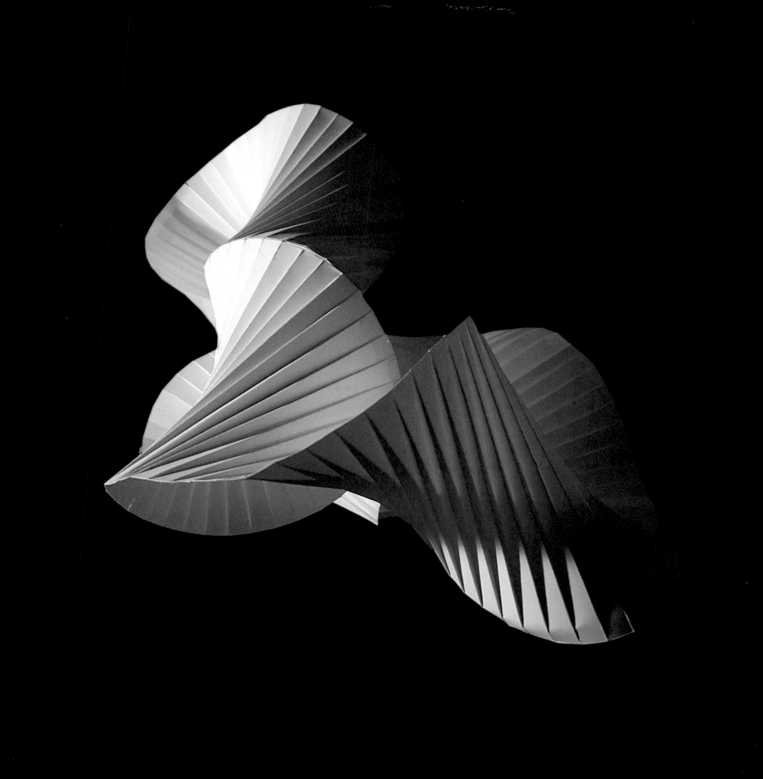

PAPER

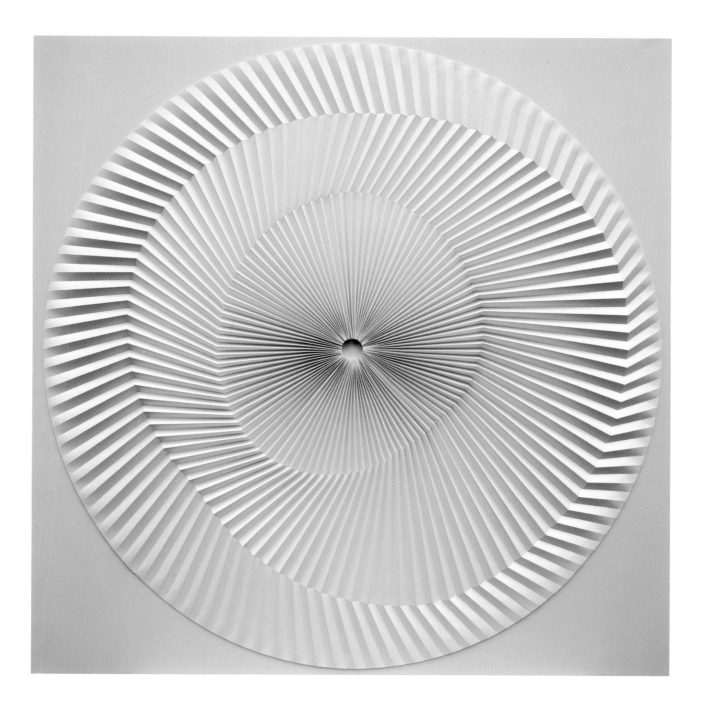

YUKO NISHIMURA

INGRID SILIAKUS

Ingrid Siliakus first witnessed the elegance of paper architecture through the work of Professor Masahiro Chatani, Japanese architect and originator of the art form. Her work includes both the reconstruction of architect's buildings and abstract sculptures, and is inspired by artists such as MC Escher, and architects such as Berlage and Gaudi.

Before the final design is finished, some 20 to 30 prototypes are constructed. Layer upon layer of drawings are added to each other until they are ready to be cut and folded as separate prototypes. Working with paper, Ingrid says, forces her to be humble, since the medium has a character of its own that asks for cooperation. "Paper architecture does not tolerate haste," she explains, "and will only respond to an approach of meditative precision." The evidence is in the contemplative character of the results.

OPPOSITE & ABOVE
Innerrings
2006
Cut paper
30 x 30 x 30 cm

OVERLEAF LEFT
Reflection on Sagrada Familia
2008
60 x 30 x 30 cm

OVERLEAF RIGHT
Captured
2008
Cut paper
30 x 25 x 25 cm
www.ingrid-siliakus.exto.org

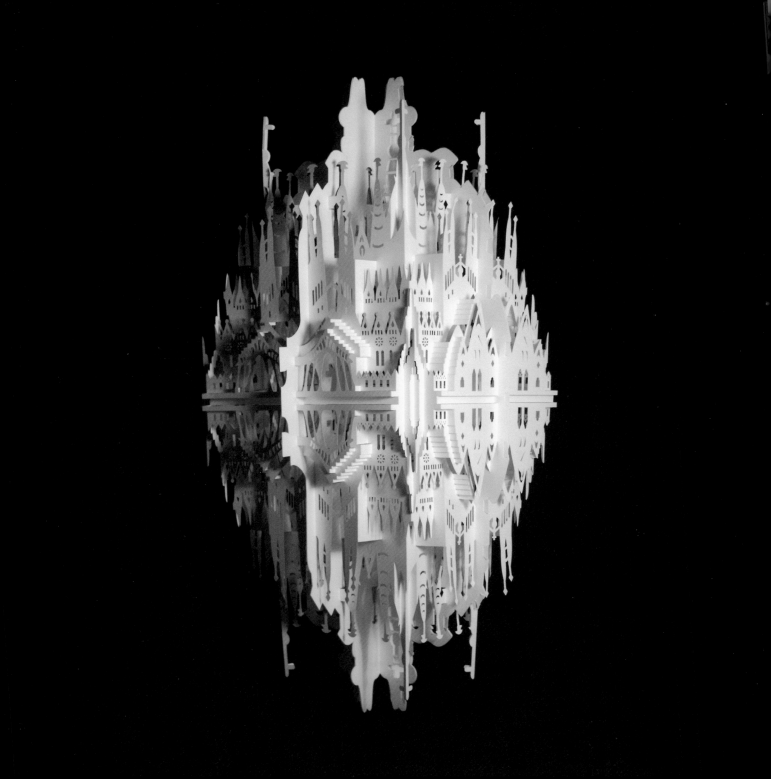

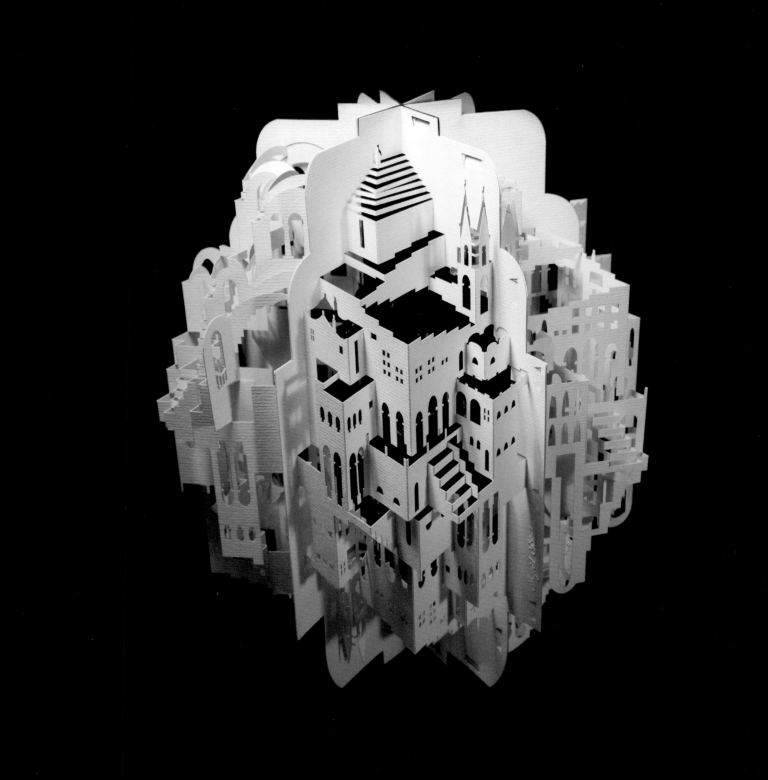

PETER CALLESEN

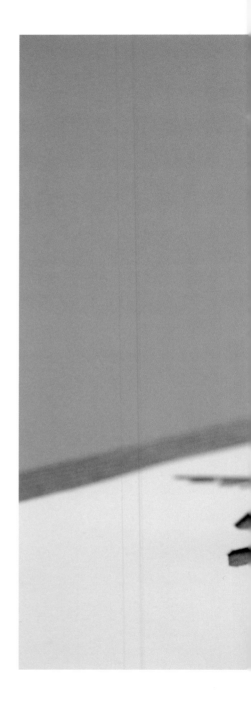

Beauty, fragility and failure are themes that lie at the heart of the work of Peter Callesen, where through delicate and highly complex paper cuts the seemingly impossible is articulated as real. Callesen's powerful poetic universe literally lifts out of the page and into life, its subject matter focusing on the grotesque and melancholic. Each paper work is an exceptional example of meticulous technique executed within a deliberately limited language of cut and fold applied to single sheets of A4 paper. The occasional application of glue aside, Callesen does not deviate from this self-imposed rule.

   Peter Callesen was born in 1967 in Denmark. His paper artworks have increasingly been receiving international attention and have featured in several shows. He currently lives and works in Copenhagen.

Distant Wish (detail)
2006
Acid-free A4 115gsm paper and glue

PAPER

OPPOSITE
Distant Wish
2006

ABOVE
The Short Distance Between
Time and Shadow
2006
Acid-free A4 115gsm paper and glue

All courtesy Helene Nyborg Contemporary

YULIA BRODSKAYA

Driven by a passion to unite illustration with typography, Yulia Brodskaya eventually developed a unique style that embraced paper cutting and folding to bring type to life.

Born in Russia, Brodskaya studied in Moscow while producing decorative fine art, then moved to London in 2004 to earn an MA in Graphic Communication. She was elected a member of the International Society of Typographic Designers in 2006 in recognition of her typographic achievement, but still practised her art primarily for pleasure. It was not until the telecommunications company Orange selected a number of her illustrations to be used across different media that she decided to focus on establishing herself as an illustrator. She has subsequently worked for many companies including Red Bull, *The Guardian*, and others. In August 2008 she submitted the winning design for the Red Bull Air Race Trophy.

Bon Apetit
2008
Courtesy the artist/www.artyulia.com

OPPOSITE
Look Good
2008

ABOVE
Yulia
2008

LEFT
City
2008

Courtesy the artist/www.artyulia.com

CLAIRE BREWSTER

Claire Brewster paraphrases Kurt Vonnegut's *Slaughter House Five* to capture her work aesthetic as "trying to construct a life that made sense from things she found in charity shops and carboot sales". For her, the artist, as an outsider, is ideally placed to pick up that which has been thrown out. Her work is about retrieving the discarded, celebrating the unwanted and giving new life to the obsolete.

A nostalgic fascination with 'things' from another place or time and a desire to examine the overlooked feeds her creativity. Believing that there is as much to learn from what society throws out as what it puts in its museums, Claire works from this starting point to create beautiful, intricate and desirable works that are greater than the sum of their parts.

Claire cuts her entomological installations from maps and atlases that are rendered obsolete by the ever-changing borders of countries. The birds, insects and flower cut-outs represent the transcendence of borders; they pass freely between countries and are then captured by Claire and put into shadow boxes to form records of past times.

Claire grew up in Lincolnshire, where it is possible to see for miles without interruption. To fill these peaceful yet bleak empty landscapes she began to create her own artistic world; she now lives and works in London and finds her inspiration from the urban environment.

Flocking
2008
Foam board, pins, box frame
100 x 76 cm

Swallow (detail from 'Oh the Birds')
2008
Cut world map, pins
Dimensions variable

KAKO UEDA

Japanese artist Kako Ueda was attracted to paper both
because of its history and its distinctive appearance.
Interested in the way in which the paper cut both
resembles a drawing yet has a three-dimensional
physicality, Ueda marries this traditional technique
with her contemporary concerns: the nature of the
organism, from the insect to the human body, and how
this natural phenomenon of existence is constantly
being influenced by culture. In her works she brings out
these concerns through an exploitation of the positive
and negative spaces her paper cuts create.

The thought-process behind Ueda's art begins
from a focus on the organic body as an ecosystem,
based both on the philosophy of ancient Chinese
medicine and the Greek philosophy of the macro-
and microcosm. Her experiments with scale, where the
minute details of the paper cut contrast with the vast
spread of her installations, are just one explicit way in
which she captures this apparent conflict visually.

ABOVE
PJS (Portrait Series I)
2006
Hand-cut paper with acrylic
71 x 46 cm

OPPOSITE
Gaze
2005
Watercolour on hand-cut black paper
51 x 36 cm
Courtesy George Adams Gallery

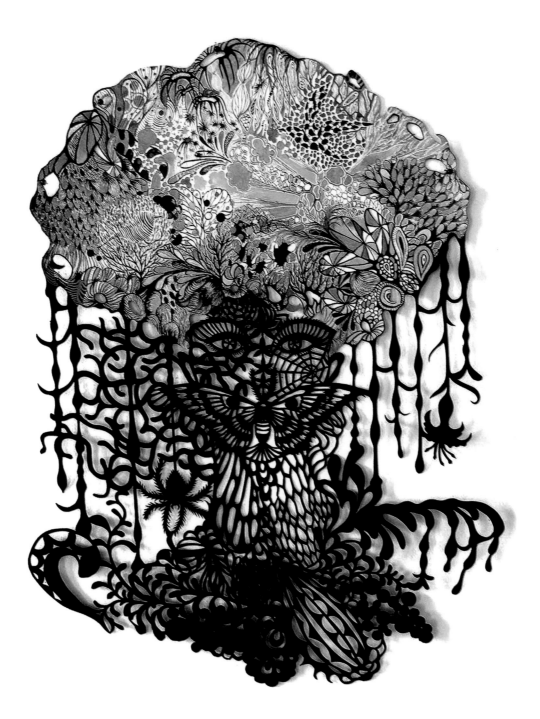

LYNDI SALES

Through intricate interweaving cuts in paper and card, Lyndi Sales laces together delicate works that explore the complexities of fate and human vulnerability. Using universally recognisable symbols of chance such as playing cards and lottery tickets, Sales employs collage and cutting to create works that operate on both small and vast scales, exploring human nature in the face of the improbable and the unpredictable.

The body of work '1 in 11,000000 Chances', from which the works here are taken, uses as its initial point of departure the 1987 Heidelberg plane crash and the political context in which it occurred. The result is a complex form that re-emerges from what Sales calls a 'detritus' as a life-like organism embodying the capricious nature of existence.

Lyndi Sales was trained at the University of Cape Town, receiving a BA in Fine Art in 1995 and an MA in 2000, both with distinction. She currently lives and works in Cape Town and exhibits widely.

OPPOSITE
Lottery Globe
2006
Paper and pins
100 x 100 cm

OVERLEAF LEFT
King of Clubs
2006
Card
30 x 30 cm

OVERLEAF RIGHT
Queen of Diamonds
2006
Card
30 x 30 cm

JEN STARK

Fractals, wormholes, MRI scans, and anatomical textbooks—the canon of inspiration that defines the paper art of Jen Stark is as unique as the work itself. Vibrant blooms of colour that burst out of pure white surfaces, Stark's pieces build layer upon layer of coloured paper and card, which are then bent out into dazzling and slightly unsettling shapes.

Stark drew inspiration from her sister, a doctor, who often brought home textbooks filled with anatomical cross-sections. She found their content and 'flip book'-style presentation both mesmerising and grotesque, and attempted to capture that reaction in her paper sculptures. At the same time, her scientific interests are also reflected in the content of her works—the piece *Coriolis Effect*, featured here, is named after the force that rotates natural systems such as hurricanes. The mathematical accuracy of the work belies the simple process of their creation, hand-cut from card using only an X-Acto knife.

OPPOSITE
Coriolis Effect
2007
Hand-cut stack of cardstock paper
30 x 30 cm

OVERLEAF LEFT
Over and Out
2008
Hand-cut stack of cardstock paper
48 x 48 cm

OVERLEAF RIGHT
Primaries: Red
2007
Hand-cut stack of cardstock paper
30 x 30 cm

Photos: Harlan Erskine

CHRIS NATROP

Los Angeles-based artist Chris Natrop brings a unique approach to the traditional art practice of paper cutting. Using a standard utility knife and rolls of high-grade drawing paper, Natrop cuts large suspended works and site-specific installations without a predetermined drawing or pattern. The results are aerial drawings with a sculptural and monumental presence, often referencing multiple natural and urban environments simultaneously. The spontaneous approach to the cut lends a freedom to the patterns, which exhibit a structural complexity that overwhelms the paper, and the environment in which they exist.

 Chris Natrop has exhibited widely throughout the United States and Europe, and was the 2007 Pulse Prize recipient from the Pulse New York art fair. He received his BFA from the School of the Art Institute of Chicago in 1993.

Black Black Butterfly Sparkle Bomb 2–4
2006
Glitter nail polish on cut black paper
with crystal ear studs
Sizes vary
Installation view Skestos Gabriele Gallery, Chicago

White White Mayday in mustard and Gold
2006
Watercolour and white tape on cut white
paper with thread and nylon netting
Site-specific installation for RAID Projects,
Los Angeles, CA

ROB RYAN

BELOW
Black on Clouds

OPPOSITE
Where You Are

Courtesy the artist

Rob Ryan's magical paper cuts and screenprints have been used by designer Paul Smith, appeared on a *Vogue* model and graced book covers including *The Book of Lost Things* by John Connolly and *The World to Come* by Dara Horn. His works touch on the romantic realms of thoughts and dreams, loneliness and longing, the personal and the universal.

Rob Ryan has been cutting pictures out of paper for many years. His technique is simple—each cut is produced using a scalpel and paper. Having exhibited all over the world, he is probably most famous for his paper dress, which featured in *Vogue*. His work is becoming increasingly sought after, both on a small and large scale.

WON PARK

Won Park was born in Korea and emigrated to the United States in 1975. Having practised origami folding for over 30 years, he has taken the skill taught to him in childhood and developed them into a unique style. He has recently become well known for his contemporary take on traditional origami subject-matter, using single dollar bills to create miniature sculptures of extraordinary complexity.

The koi fish featured was inspired by a watercolour painting he saw while eating in a Chinese restaurant. The incorporation of the original design on the dollar bill into the final work gives the koi an added graphic dimension.

Koi
2008
Folded dollar bill

DAN McPHARLIN

The inspiration behind Dan McPharlin's 'Analogue Miniatures' series lies in his parallel work in sound art and electronic music. These tiny models of fictional synthesizers and recording equipment were inspired by Japanese capsule toys and the vintage aesthetic of cluttered analogue control panels.

As an independent artist and designer, he has produced work for record sleeves, magazines, books and websites, and has exhibited his work in Australia and overseas.

Dan McPharlin was born in Adelaide, Australia in 1977. After studying Visual Arts at the University of South Australia he has worked independently for clients as broad as *The New York Times*, *Wallpaper*, *Esquire*, *Warp Records*, *Stones Throw* and the Chicago Museum of Contemporary Art.

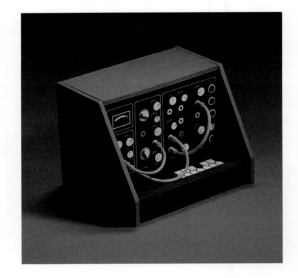

Models from 'Analogue Miniatures' series
Courtesy Dan McPharlin
www.danmcpharlin.com

PIERRE VANNI

Pierre Vanni is an emerging French graphic designer working with paper and card. He founded his studio in 2007 and has already had work featured in the Centre George Pompidou in Paris, *The New York Style* magazine, *Dazed and Confused*, *Grafik* and *IdN*.

His folds are both playful and sculptural. *Reflet* and *Archimede* exhibit a complex approach to relief folding, in contrast to other, less abstract works he has become known for, including a more tongue-in-cheek series of rabbits and a distinctive folded skull.

Pierre Vanni draws on a diverse range of influences, from the works of Renaissance painters such as Hans Holbein, to the writings of Tanizaki Junichiro, who distills the aesthetic qualities of the ordinary in everyday Japanese life in his book *In Praise of Shadows*. Vanni is particularly indebted to the Japanese aesthetic and is inspired not only by Japanese design but also poetry, citing Hideki Inaba or Nagi Noda as sources of inspiration. This can be witnessed in his delicate, minimalist approach to paper relief.

ABOVE
Reflet
June 2008
Produced for Manystuff
Photo: Julien Lelièvre

OPPOSITE
Archimede
September 2008
Produced for Regala
Photo: Pierre Vanni

RIKI MOSS

For Riki Moss, light brings revelation, and in her
Studio Glow installation it serves to illuminate,
literally, the fine grain details of the piece's dynamic
structure and variegated skin. Light is diffused through
the paper along pathways within the fibre plane of
the paper itself, creating the contrasting shadow tones
that show the topographical character of the surface
in high relief.

Each piece evokes associations with natural
forms that have served as inspiration for the works:
the ribbed under-structures of plant and animal
bodies, the curl of breaking waves, and wind-
sculpted sandstone formations. The works themselves
meanwhile emulate the effects of these natural forces.

Moss's formations are created from Manilla Hemp
Abaca paper, which is overbeaten for seven or eight
hours in a Hollander beater to allow for maximum
shrinkage; the embedded materials allow for self-
supporting structures.

Studio Glow
2008
Installation
Manilla Hemp Abaca paper

EMILY MORRIS

Mister Charlesworth is a commissioned installation
of laser-cut paper panels by textile designer Emily
Morris, produced for Chiltern Street Studio, London.
The panels feature insect imagery that has been
transformed into intricate lace-like cut paper designs.
The work touches on the idea of making something
usually unpleasant into something of beauty. Initially
viewers are not aware of what is hidden within the
floral design; it is only when viewed closer that the
true nature of the insect's infestation is revealed.

The patterns were laser-cut and etched into the
paper. Individual insects and other curiosities also
cut from paper were then left at the installation site
and visitors were encouraged to attach them to the
installation. Gradually the patterns began to develop
each day, as if an infestation was taking over. This
creative interaction between the viewer and the
installation meant that the design was constantly
evolving, resulting in a unique visual display.

Detail from *Mister Charlesworth*
2007
Laser-cut paper installation
Produced for Chiltern Street Studio, London

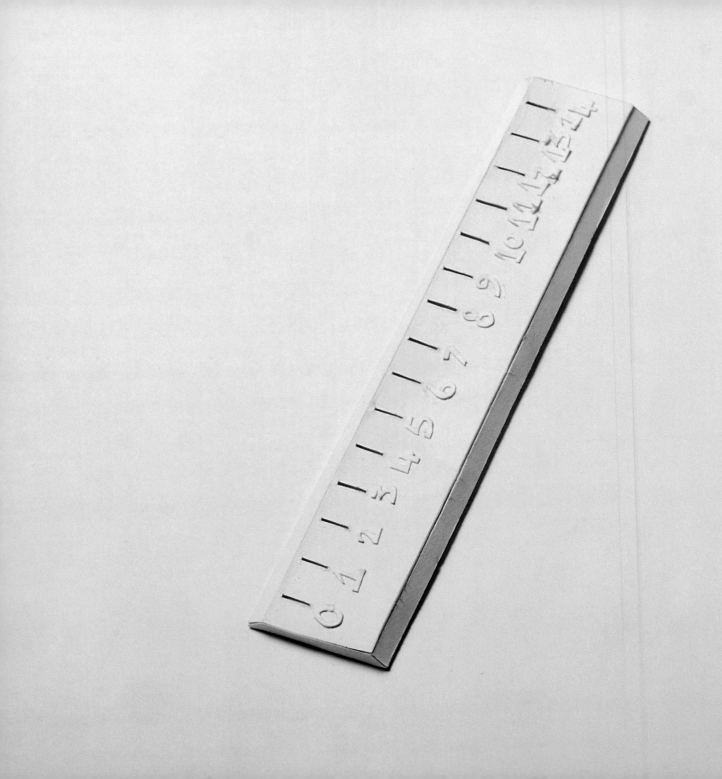

BOOK
ART

CARA BARER

A random encounter on Drew Street with a discarded Houston *Yellow Pages* was the primary inspiration for Cara Barer's *Books Project*. After photographing the book on a pavement, Barer began to search for more books, and more methods to manipulate their appearance.

For Barer, the project is about blurring the line between object, sculpture, and photography. Her starting point is the content of each volume, which has a varying impact on the final work—the *New Century Dictionary of the English Language*, for example, was defined by its fascinating illustrations and archaic visual content. Barer's sculpting segued to thoughts on obsolescence and the relevance of libraries in this century.

The photographs here are a lament for the passing of an era when books were considered more valuable, and a path to knowledge. Today, they are disposable and have largely been replaced by the internet as a primary source of information. *The Books Project* hopes to raise questions about these changes, and the transient and fragile nature in which we now choose to obtain knowledge, as well as the future of books.

All images: *The Books Project*
Courtesy the artist

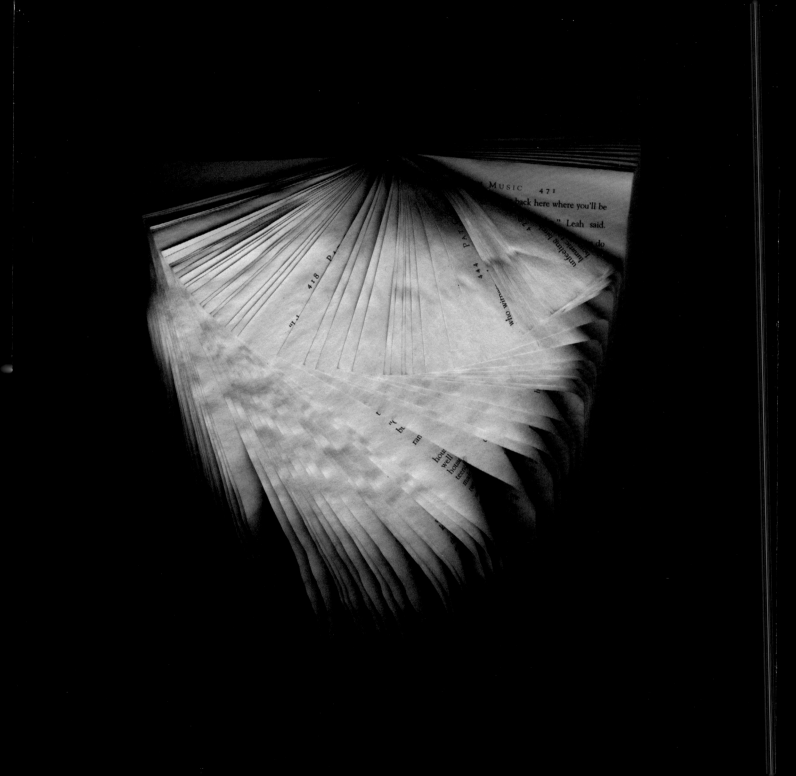

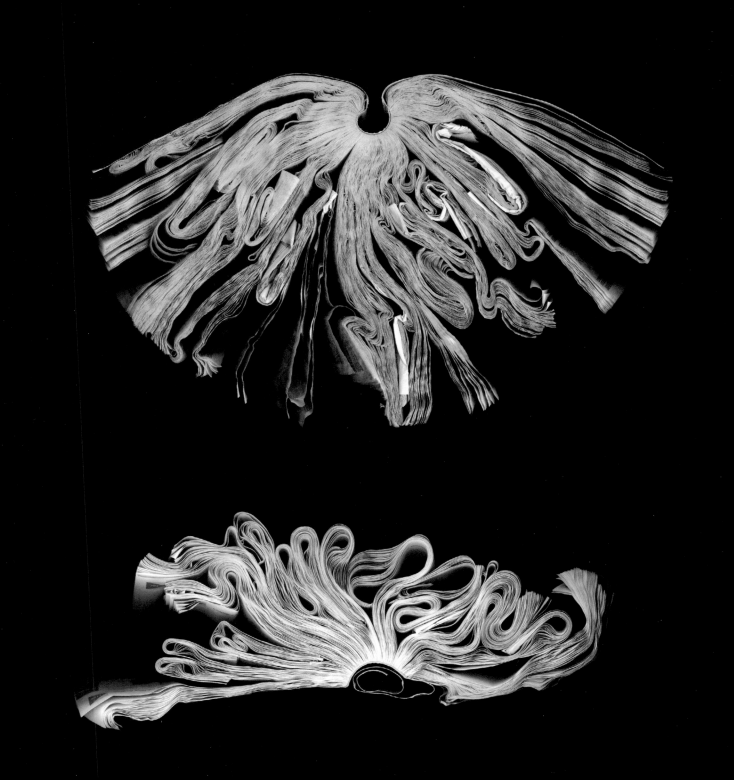

GEORGIA RUSSELL

Using a scalpel in place of a brush or a pen, Georgia Russell creates complex constructions that transform found ephemera, such as books, music scores, maps, newspapers, currency and photographs. Slicing up books and placing them in specimen jars, Russell's carefully chosen objects take on the character of organic forms immortalised in glass. Era-defining books and groundbreaking philosophical texts, such as Ernst Gombrich's *The Story of Art*, Germaine Greer's *The Female Eunuch*, and Marcel Raymond's *De Baudelaire au Surrealisme*, feature in Russell's systematic, explosive deconstructions, creating a unique library of literary decimation.

Georgia Russell's work was featured in the exhibition 'Persistent Obsessions' in 2008 at the London gallery England & Co, and has further solo shows forthcoming.

PAPER

Con
2008
Altered book and digital video
Music by Dmitry Pavlovsky

Chronic
2008
Altered book and digital video
Music by Dmitry Pavlovsky

BRIAN DETTMER

Artist Brian Dettmer has developed a unique approach to cutting up and reconstructing books in order to create artworks with conceptual resonance. *Chronicle, Chronic, Con* is an installation comprised of three altered books with three accompanying videos. The three pieces are originally derived from the same book, *The Chronicle of the Twentieth Century* (published by Chronicle Publications, Inc.), but each intervention takes a unique path. When installed the books hang a few feet apart from each other on one wall and the corresponding videos are projected on the wall opposite the books. In each piece, a still image was taken after every layer was removed and then animated to create a time lapse video which illustrates the process and questions the validity of linear time, memory and recorded history. Each video is created from over 3,000 still shots of the pieces in progress and the total installation contains over 10,000 unique images.

Dettmer's more compact work *Brave New World* is a construction built from 14 copies in nine different editions. Separated into two hemispheres they suggest a split globe or the hemispheres of a brain. Each side is treated in the same manner and each book contains the same text, but every fragment of text is unique. Nothing is moved or added to the text, which has been carved into and edited only through the process of removal. Through this process, narratives become ideas, ideas become memories and memories become isolated fragments.

Brian Dettmer was born in 1974, and trained at Columbia College in Chicago, studying Art and Design and Art History. He now lives and works in Atlanta.

PAPER

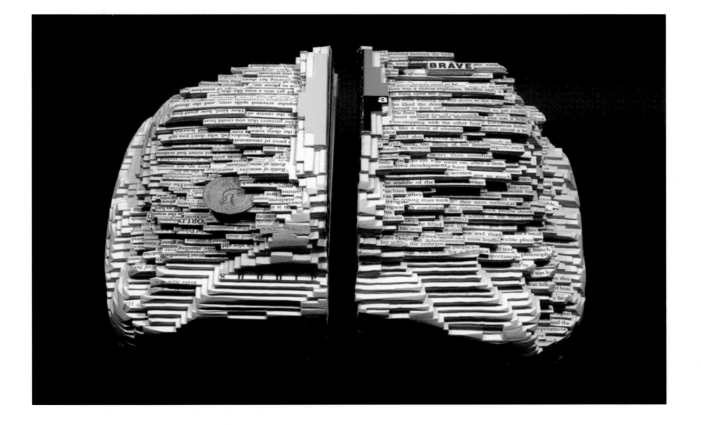

Brave New World
2008
Altered books
14.5 x 30.5 cm

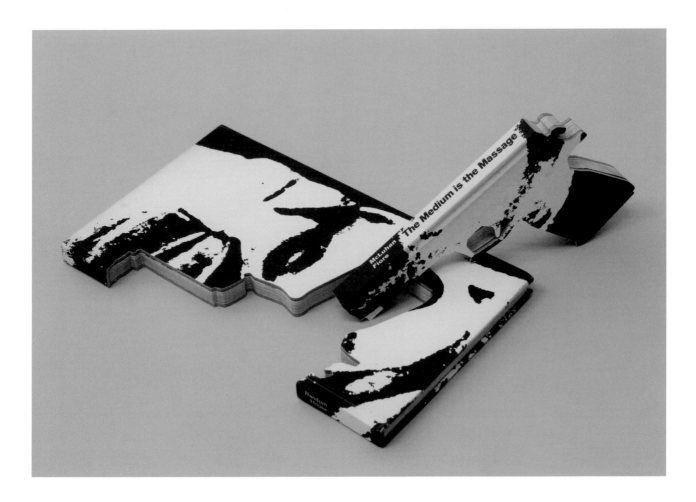

The Medium is the Message
2006

ROBERT THE

Artist Robert The takes both a playful and deeply philosophical approach to his book cuts. "Obsession with the semiotic erosion of meaning and reality," he explains, "has led me to create objects that evangelise their own relevance by a direct fusion of word and form. Books (many culled from dumpsters and thrift store bins) are lovingly vandalised back to life so they can assert themselves against the culture which turned them into debris."

One of his most distinctive works, the *Desert Rose* series is a modular construction consisting of cut-up King James Bibles, which in its largest form has been put together using a total of 60 Bibles. The assemblage is not straightforward, and the result gives off the illusion of an impossible interlocking chain. The basis of the *Desert Rose* recalls the expansive structures of modular origami.

Born in Carmel, California, in 1961, Robert The studied philosophy and mathematics at the University of Wisconsin, Madison, and moved on to the Institute of Lettering and Design in Chicago in 1986. He began making book pieces in 1991. He currently lives in Kingston, New York.

ROBERT THE   125

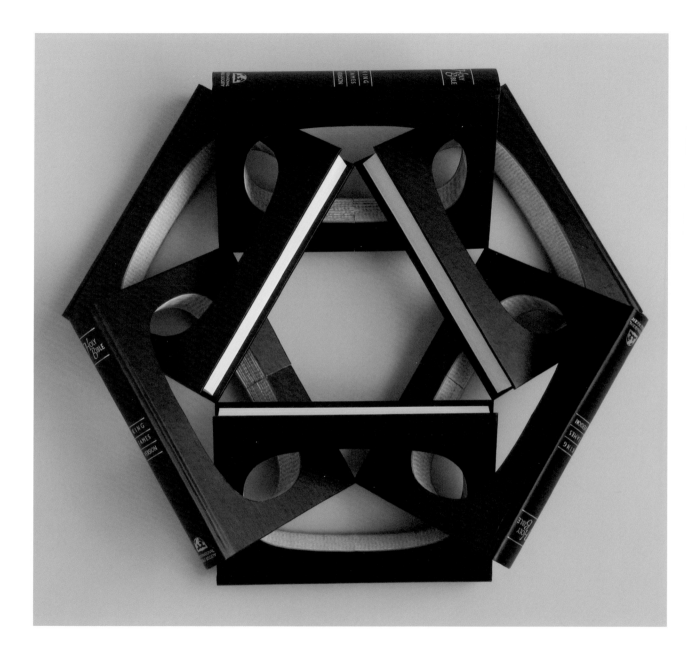

PAPER

OPPOSITE
Desert Rose
2006

ABOVE
Braque
2006
Collection of Allan Chasanoff

Photos: Robert The

ELLEN BELL

Ellen Bell's paper work, though driven by concepts surrounding communication and the written and spoken word, remains firmly grounded in a craft tradition that pays homage to the process of fine needlework.

Her current series of works are text-on-paper 'forms' and 'drawings', all meticulously constructed using original pages from dictionaries, phrase books, thesauri and classic works of literature. Formal page layouts are reconstructed by fixing the cut-out words in carefully measured columns that read as stream-of-consciousness lists peppered with archaic, long-lost phraseology. The undulating spiral of text in *Conversations 2007* represents the physical flow of words and memories, while also operating as a physical artefact of communication.

The language books that Ellen chose for 'Speaking Soul' are exclusively utilitarian in their aesthetic, selected from the late 1890s to the 1950s to emphasise the fact that language has historical baggage. The books symbolise the hurdles which non-English speakers have to overcome to become able to participate emotionally with the culture in which they find themselves.

After training as a theatre designer, Bell enjoyed a varied career as a photographic stylist, costume and model-maker before returning to education to take a degree in illustration, and an MA in Fine Art. She has since featured in various notable national and international art fairs such as COLLECT at the Victoria & Albert Museum and SOFA in Chicago.

Conversations 2007 from 'Speaking Soul'
2007
Installation at the City Gallery in Leicester
Photos: Stephen Lynch

SU BLACKWELL

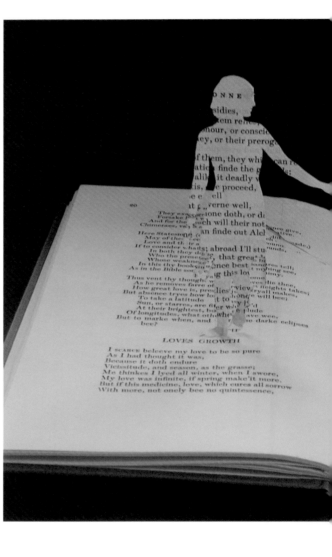

The work of Su Blackwell is all about transformation. She takes an object of value and de-values it by cutting through it or tearing it up. Using the familiar, she creates the fantastical; non-art materials such as books and clothes are taken and reimagined to form works that evoke a sense of dreamy melancholy or magical enchantment.

Su Blackwell's interest in the realm of fairy-tales and folk legends has led her to focus on a series of works constructed from books that explore these themes, externalising the stories from the pages of the book and allowing them to be read in an alternative way. These works can be seen as metaphors for language, operating in a way that is both powerful and ephemeral.

The Extasie
2006
Cut-up book
Courtesy the artist

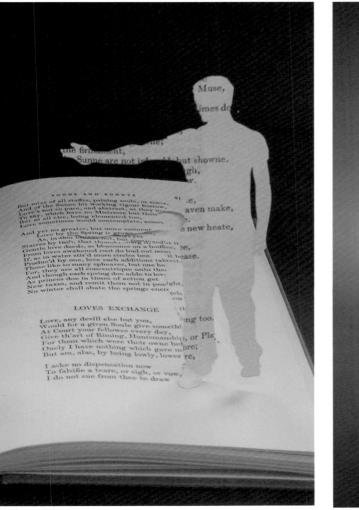

The Elder Tree Mother
2007
Cut-up book
Courtesy the artist

SELINA SWAYNE

A collaboration between Selina Swayne and Hanna Bayatti, *No Title* started as a visual study of nothingness in man-made spaces. Selina Swayne's photographs depict a concrete wilderness built out of transitory places captured on film. On the reverse, the real and the unreal are merged in Hanna Bayatti's collages of interior spaces. The result is a curious and uncertain exploration of the misplaced purpose of different environments. The design of the book, a concertina in which the cross-sections between the illustration and photographs were removed, produces a second outcome—a theatrical world with no boundaries. The book delves into the idea that space does not necessarily need a function to be understood.

Selina Swayne in collaboration with Hanna Bayatti
No Title
2008
Book from cut photographs

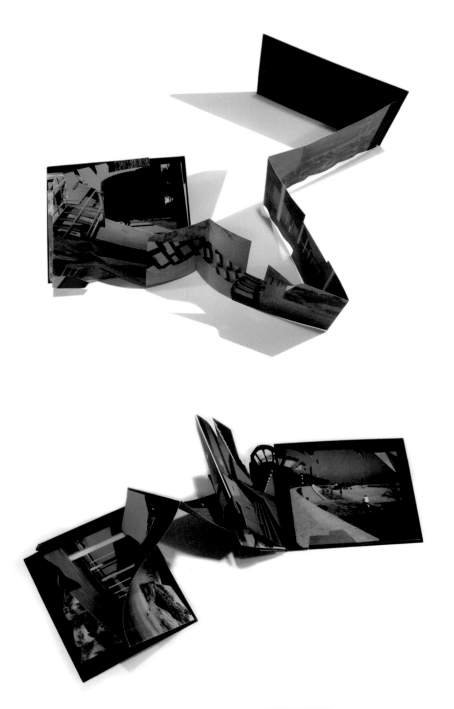

NORIKO AMBE
ED RUSCHA

On the subject of her paper cuts, Noriko Ambe has emphasised the role of process in creating meaning: "Time is essential to my work. Because over time I add more and more paper to a sculpture, the work itself ends up embodying the time taken to create it. The process is as important as the finished product." She recalls an inspirational moment: "Once, when I was in an airplane, I saw a beautiful sea of clouds below me that made me want to melt into the natural world. In the topographies that I cut into paper, human life merges with nature and all boundaries are dissolved."

Here, that aesthetic is merged with the book art of American artist Ed Ruscha. For further examples of her work, see pp. 34–39.

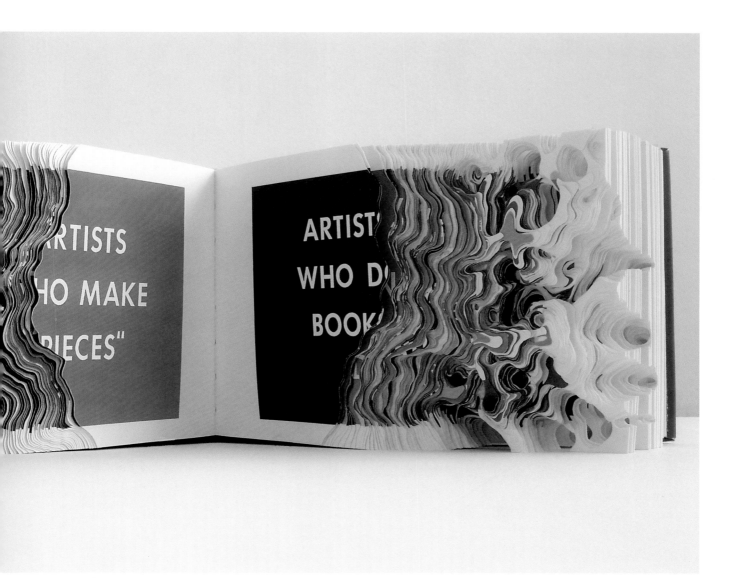

Artists who make Pieces, Artists who do Books
2008
From Cutting Book Series with Ed Ruscha
13 x 37 x 20 cm

THOMAS ALLEN

American artist Thomas Allen has taken a knife to the pulp novel and recreated it by literally folding out the cover illustrations to create three-dimensional montages. In *Recoil*, an incision cuts straight through the book like a bullet, while *Viewfinder* depicts a man peering surreptitiously from behind a book spine at two women in a state of undress. The cover of *Spill the Jackpot* meanwhile, literally 'spills' out of the spine. Each work uses the content of the book to drive the character of the work, the combination of cheek and pulp pastiche bringing a fresh dimension to Allen's extensive collection of cult novels.

His work can be found in the collections of the University of St Francis, Milwaukee Museum of Art and Minneapolis Institute of Arts, amongst others.

ABOVE
Fury
2006
51 x 64 cm
Chromogenic print

OPPOSITE
Recoil
2006
64 x 51 cm
Chromogenic print

Courtesy Foley Gallery

ABOVE
Viewfinder
2006
64 x 51 cm
Chromogenic print

OPPOSITE
Jackpot
2006
51 x 64 cm
Chromogenic print

TAKESHI ISHIGURO

Takeshi Ishiguro's *Book of Light* is a book in outward appearance. Open it, however, and an illuminated pop-up lamp emerges. Lit by three small LEDs and powered by a low-voltage adapter, the light is subtle but atmospheric, with the emphasis on style over functionality. Placed on a flat surface, it makes for a coffee table with unusually illuminating content.

Takeshi was born in Japan in 1969 and completed an Industrial Design course at the Royal College of Art in London. He worked for IDEO in both the USA and Japan from 1996 until 2002, at which point he began working on his own. His design work has featured in the permanent collection of the New York Museum of Modern Art since 1998. *The Book of Light* is available to purchase through Artecnica.

Book of Light
2008
Designed for Artecnica

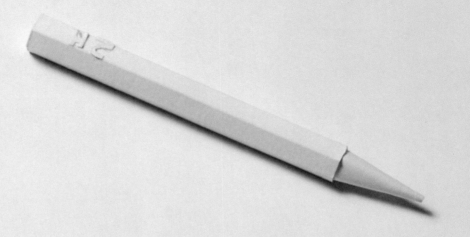

MICHAEL CEPRESS

Commissioned by Greek cultural organisation ATOPOS
for their 2006 exhibition showcasing fashion created
from paper, Michael Cepress's series 'Collars for the
Modern Gentleman' uses the *Yellow Pages* directory to
create a tongue-in-cheek fashion item.

'Collars...' is reflective of Cepress's fascination
with menswear and the tailoring tradition which drives
his work, and has led him to write extensively on
fashion's relationship to gender and popular culture.
In 2005, his debut menswear collection was featured
in the sold-out runway show 'Michael Cepress Presents
An Evening of Men's Fashion'. He has subsequently
been a 2007 nominee for the Louis Comfort Tiffany
Foundation Art Award. His work has appeared in a
2008 exhibition alongside John Galliano, Issey Miyake,
Hussein Chalayan (see pp. 152–153) and Walter
Van Beirendonck.

Michael Cepress received his BA in Art from the
University of Wisconsin–Green Bay and his Master
of Fine Arts degree in Fibres from the University
of Washington.

Collar for the Modern Gentleman
with a Yellow Pages Dress
2006
Commissioned by ATOPOS
Photos: Michelle Moore

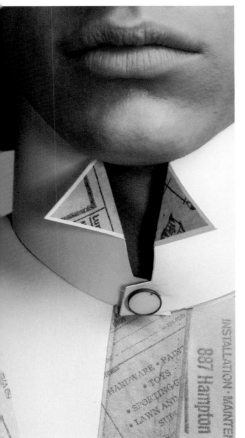

GARY HARVEY

Fashion designer Gary Harvey takes familiar everyday icons and recontextualises them within the world of high fashion couture. His experiments with 'eco-couture' are a direct response to the waste he has seen occurring in the fashion business. The *Recycled Paper Dress*, one of a series of dresses from recycled materials, is made from 30 copies of the *Financial Times* newspaper. Other unique creations have used bottle-tops, cartons, plastic bags and even Burberry macs.

The decision to use recycled materials to create couture initially came about almost by accident: the idea to create a dress from 42 pairs of Levi 501s followed an attempt to source a dramatic garment for one of his photo shoots.

Harvey trained at Ravensbourne College and the Royal College of Art in London. Following a ten-year career as the creative director behind Levi and Dockers brand-advertising images, he then returned to the roots of craftsmanship in fashion to develop his unique style.

Recycled Paper Dress
2007
Eco-Couture made from 30 copies
of the *Financial Times* newspaper
Art Direction: Gary Harvey
Photo: Robert Decelis
Model: Tabitha Hall, courtesy of Models1

SUSAN CUTTS

The image of the 'dress' is used frequently in the work of Susan Cutts, who is driven by an intrigue both towards its historical and contemporary perception. Cutts uses her own handmade paper, working from the raw fibre and using traditional European equipment and methods.

The process of making the paper is an essential part of the work, as is the selection and preparation of the fibres, since they allow through their complex structure the creation of sculptural pieces that hold their form without the use of glue, stitching or armatures.

LEFT
Nursery Rhyme
Paper dress installation

RIGHT
Fairy Tale
Suspended paper dress

SUSAN CUTTS

PAPER

LEFT
White Paper Dress

OPPOSITE
Paper Insects

Photos: Henrik Adamsen

VIOLISE LUNN

Alongside the creation of functional evening wear, fashion designer Violise Lunn has an alternative passion—making unwearable clothing using paper as a textile. Taking the freedom allowed by paper in fashion design that other textiles cannot accommodate, Lunn's paper shoes and dresses reflect compositions that would be impossible in any other medium.

Dividing her time between these two art forms, the wearable and unwearable, useable and useless, Lunn draws inspiration from the contrast of the two, and their specific characters. While references to both the past and fantasies of the future exist in her work, the overwhelming sensation in her delicate compositions is of objects that convey a surprising and uplifting indifference to the external world.

Violise Lunn was born in Copenhagen in 1969, and graduated as a fashion designer in 1995 from Denmark Design School. She has run her own studio in Copenhagen since 1997, where she specialises in the design and making of one-of-a-kind pieces of clothing for women. In 1999 she won the Danish fur prize 'The Golden Fur Needle'. In 2000, she was awarded the 'Golden Button'. In 2002, Carlsberg gave her the 'Thimble Award'.

HUSSEIN CHALAYAN

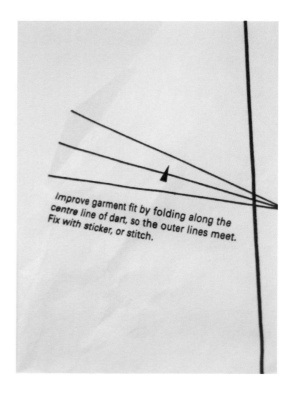

Improve garment fit by folding along the centre line of dart, so the outer lines meet. Fix with sticker, or stitch.

In 1999 Hussein Chalayan designed a unique dress —the first in a series—that could be folded flat and posted through the mail. Folding out from a simple airmail envelope, there is no waste and all the assemblage instructions are simply marked in lines on the material itself. This tongue-in-cheek creation is a simultaneous token of one's absence and presence, much like the sending of letters.

Chalayan, who has recently become creative director for cutting-edge sports brand Puma, has a visionary and pioneering approach to fashion design. Drawing upon disciplines outside the sphere of fashion and embracing the potential of modern technology, his work unites personal and global concerns.

Born in Cyprus in 1970, Chalayan moved to London where he studied at Central St Martins College of Art and Design. He launched his own label in 1994, and has since twice been named British Designer of the Year.

Airmail Dress
1999
Folded and unfolded airmail paper
Collection of Hussein Chalayan
Photos: Matthew Pull

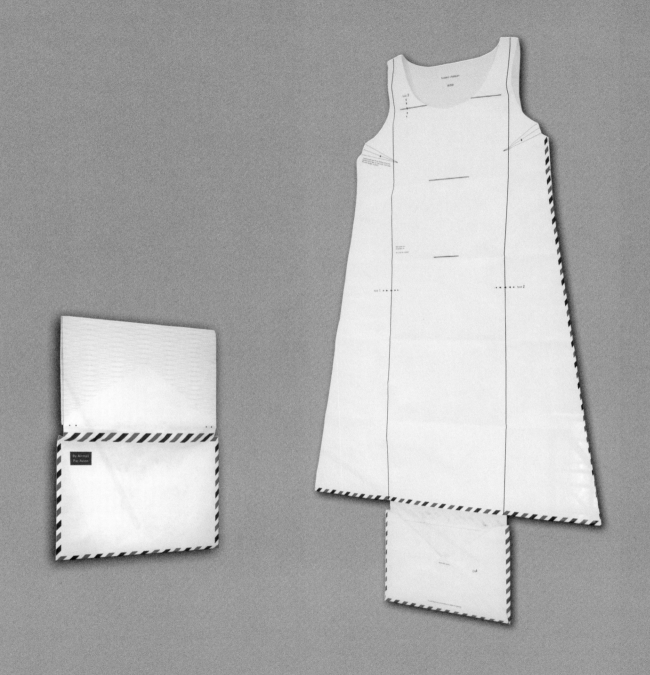

JUM NAKAO

In 2004 Brazilian designer Jum Nakao caused an international sensation at São Paulo Fashion Week when he presented 'A Costura do Invisivel' (Sewing the Invisible), a collection of ethereal dresses crafted from paper. At the end of the show, to the audible horror of the audience, the models tore off the garments, leaving 180 days of work by a team of 150 people shredded on the catwalk floor. The show created such a storm that on the tenth anniversary of São Paulo Fashion Week in 2006, officials declared 'A Costura do Invisivel' Brazil's parade of the decade.

Jum Nakao took inspiration from late-nineteenth century fashions, a period when clothing was extremely elaborate and precious both in volume and texture, these values crucial to the intense feeling of wonder that the designer wished to generate in his audience. The paper reliefs were embossed by Brazil's most traditional engraving company, Balsemão. To cut the lacework for each model, Universal laser technology was used. Jum Nakao's team selected vegetable-fibre paper in order to give a subtle transparency to the garments, and Verge de France for its toughness, suitable to the setting. To generate a sense of enchantment, the models were dressed as fairies with distinctive Playmobil-inspired hair. This playful element was designed to make it easy for the spectator to project themselves into the work, as if in a fairy tale.

OPPOSITE AND OVERLEAF
Dress from 'A Costura do Invisivel'
2004
Laser-cut paper
For São Paulo Fashion Week 2004
Photos: Sandra Bordin and Fernando Louza

PAPER

WHITE CASHMERE COLLECTION

Canadian bathroom tissue manufacturer Cashmere has
for several years held an annual fashion show featuring
dresses created from their tissue by top designers. 'The
White Cashmere Collection 2008: A Touch of Pink'
featured the original couture of eight leading Canadian
designers, each crafted in 100 per cent bathroom
tissue. The fifth annual collection also included a new,
limited-edition pink range of tissue, designed to raise
funds for the Canadian Breast Cancer Foundation. The
elegant result displays the delicacy and subtlety of paper
alongside the distinctive character of high fashion, the
folded and creased tissue performing in the manner of
the lightest of fabrics.

Thien Le
Paper dress from Cashmere
Bathroom Tissue

LEFT
David Dixon

OPPOSITE
Evan Biddell

Paper dresses from Cashmere Bathroom
Tissue, Kruger Products Canada

Designed for 'The White Cashmere
Collection 2008: A Touch of Pink'

Photos: Jason Kearns, Richard Dubois

NEL LINSSEN

Nel Linssen is not purely known for the disarming beauty of her jewellery—her innovative use of materials plays an integral role in the character of her designs. The artist's range of necklaces, bracelets and other jewellery have, since 1986, been made from a special type of cardboard known as 'trough'. She takes an empirical approach to design, seeking solutions through direct experimentation. This extensive research process has led to very deliberate choices regarding colour, cuts and folds in order to enhance the interplay of light and shade on the objects, and to guarantee a reliable structural solidity.

Linssen's work is characterised by a minimalist aesthetic aimed at harmonising the colour, volume and structure of her works within continuous, modular shapes. Although some are held together with elastic or plastic tubing, structural research has led to self-supporting designs that rely purely on the cut and fold of the paper.

The rigorous monumentality of her jewellery comes alive when it is worn, at which point the tactile pleasure of the paper comes into play. Her necklaces sit softly on the neck and her bracelets work gracefully around the wrists as they interact with ambient light.

Her work has featured in numerous solo shows, appeared in several major contemporary jewellery publications and features in public collections all over the world.

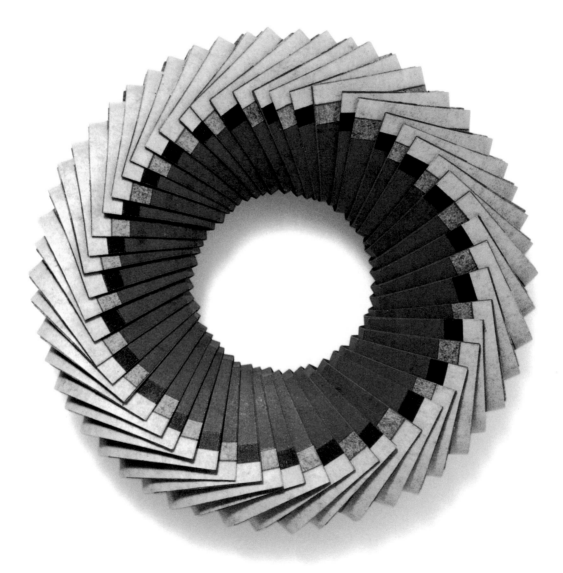

PAPER

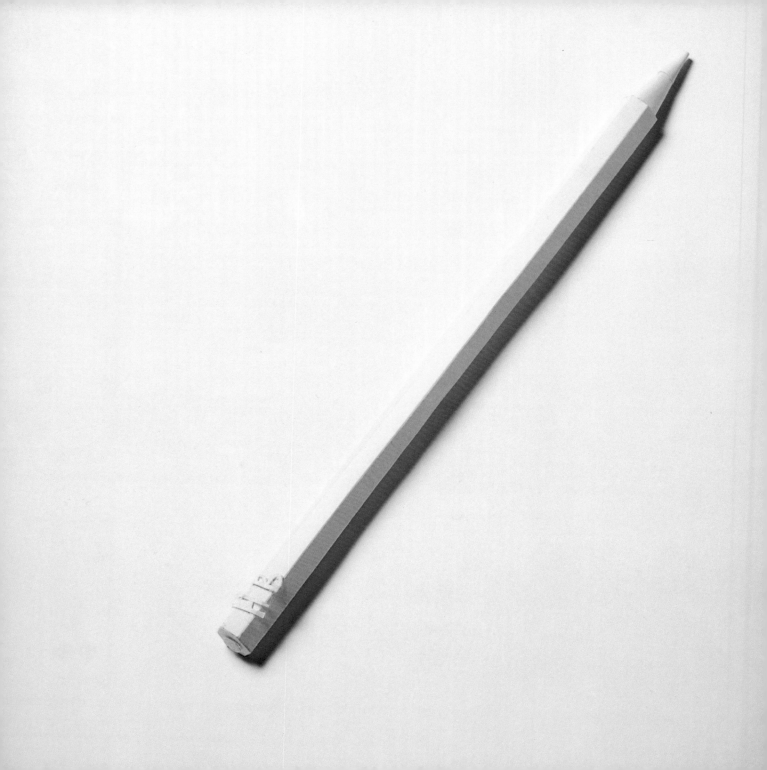

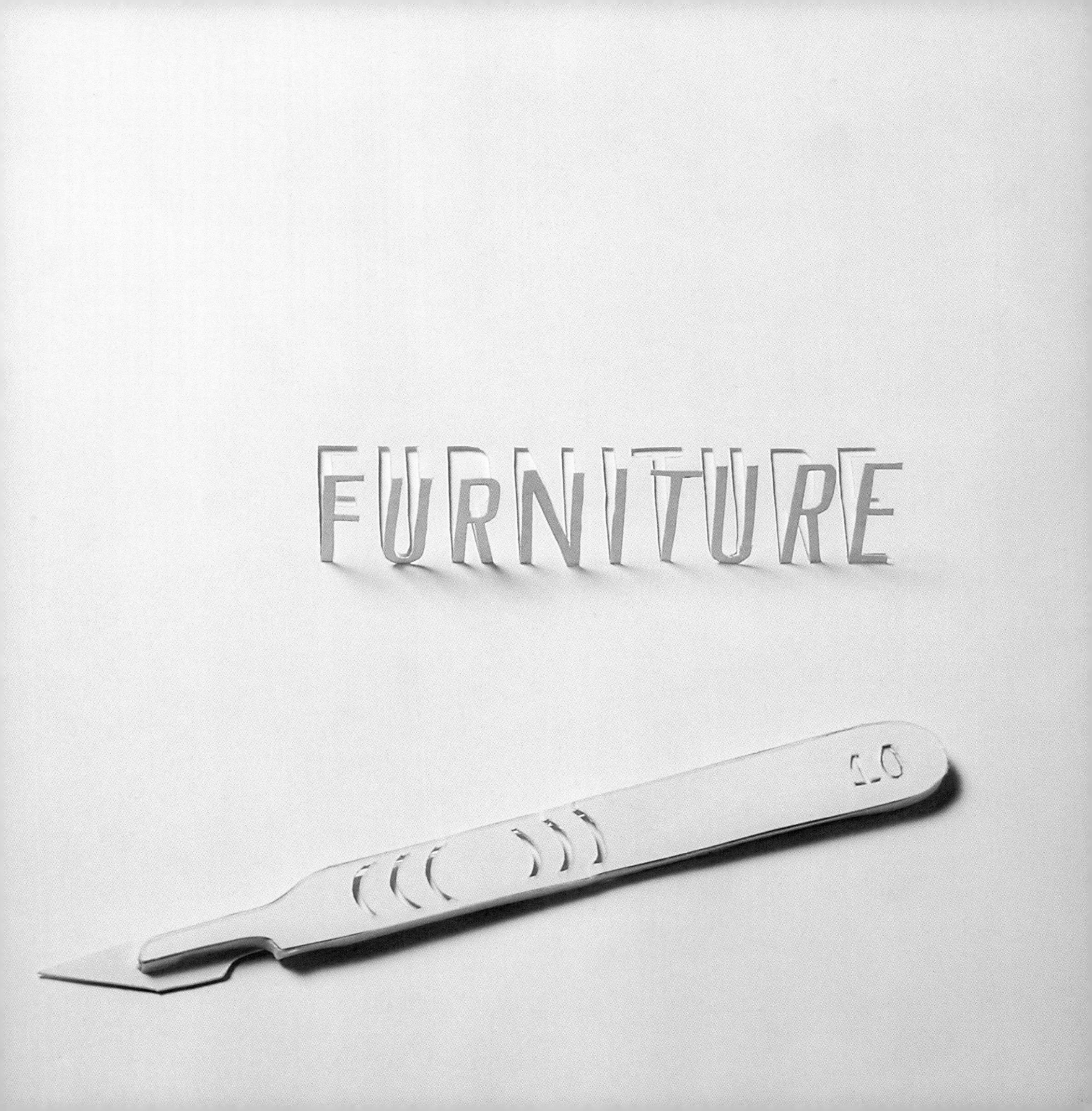
FURNITURE
10

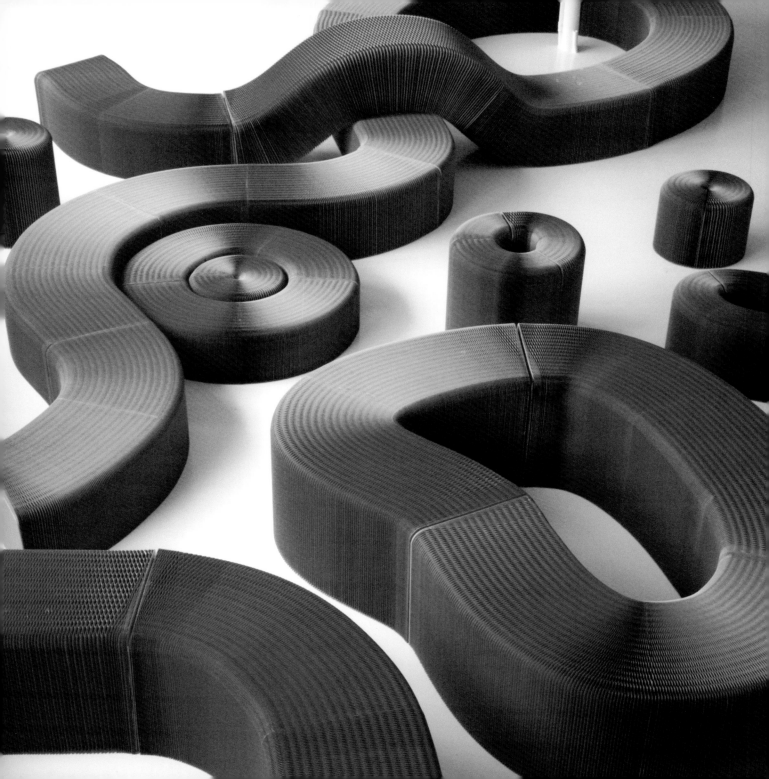

MOLO DESIGN

The concept of 'softhousing' and 'softroom' was dreamt up by molo design while they were exploring the potential of soft and flexible structures. At the time the molo design team were operating in a small one-room studio and saw the need for a furnishing design that would allow for a small private space designed for sleeping, reading or working that could be folded up when not in use, thus giving space back to the working studio.

Realising that people in cities all over the world were in the same situation, operating out of modest-sized urban apartments, molo designed 'softhousing' and 'softroom', furnishings that could be prefabricated, packed flat and installed in existing houses, apartments and studio lofts.

Alongside their furnishing range, they also founded a competition called 'Design beyond East and West' that drew attention to the issue of families living in small urban apartments. They noticed that

in this type of family apartment the common shared living space of the family was disappearing as all the space is taken by a series of bedrooms along a corridor. The idea behind 'softhousing' and 'softroom' is to allow bedrooms to be folded away when not in use— giving space back for the family to gather. Not only is softhousing and softroom effectively functional, but its relationship with its surrounding environment also has a distinctive sculptural beauty.

softhousing
2008
Flexible paper honeycomb

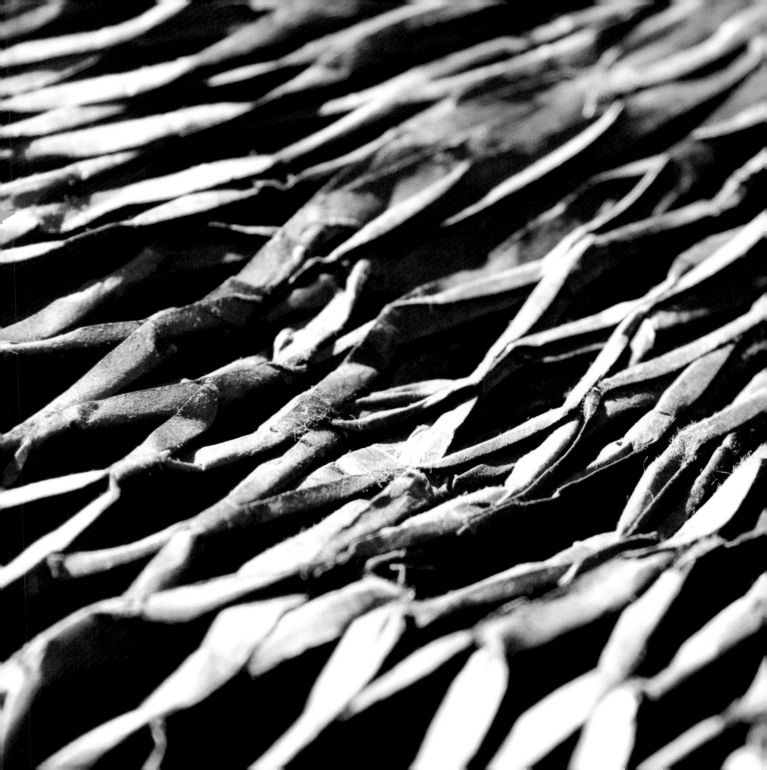

MARTI KALLIALA
ESA RUSKEEPÄÄ
MARTIN LUKASCZYK

Mafoombey was the winning entry in a design contest arranged by the University of Art and Design Helsinki and Finnish Fair Foundation in 2005. The competition brief called for a space for listening and experiencing music within a fixed set of dimensions.

The initial concept for the design developed from an ambition to create a strong spatial intensity and distinguished atmosphere within the limited volume of the given dimensions. It matured into an idea of an intuitive freeform space cut into a rectangular stack of material. The low 'resolution' of the form and the perception of weight and structure were considered key issues.

Corrugated cardboard was chosen as the construction material as it had a strong aesthetic appeal which the designers believed was yet to be fully exploited on the scale at which they intended to use it. Additional advantages of the material were value, and penetration of light and air, and most importantly,

sound. It gave excellent acoustics, which was a critical factor.

Mafoombey was designed by Marti Kalliala, Esa Ruskeepää and Martin Lukasczyk. The corporate cooperation partner in the project was Stora Enso Packaging. It was shown at the Contemporary Finnish Architecture 2004–2005 exhibition at the Museum of Finnish Architecture in 2006, was nominated for the Forum Prize 2005, and won the Habitare design contest the next year.

Mafoombey: Space for Music
2005
250 x 250 x 250 cm
Corrugated cardboard

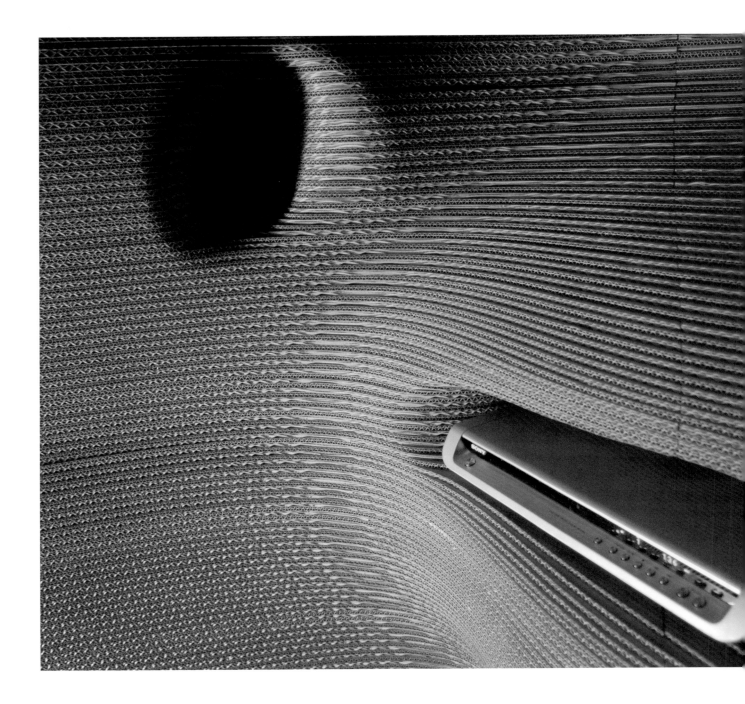

PAPER

TOKUJIN YOSHIOKA

Light and strong, the naturally-created honeycomb is ultimately a form of architecture. Tokujin Yoshioka's *Honey-pop Chair* is made with sheets of glassine paper that are piled together and cut along specific lines so that it magically opens up into a honeycomb structure. The final form of the chair is set when in use, as it responds to the body shape of the sitter.

This iconic piece of paper furnishing is now a part of the permanent collection at the Museum of Modern Art (MoMA), Vitra Design Museum, the Pompidou Centre, and the Victoria & Albert Museum.

The design aesthetic of Tokujin Yoshioka draws from the laws of nature, and with his installation with Moroso in 2007, he used this as a starting-point to focus on echoing the characteristics of snow and clouds through the organisation of a variety of natural materials. At the Moroso showroom in New York, he also covered up the entire space with approximately 30,000 sheets of tissue. Fascinated by the beauty of this silk-like paper and the way in which such a simple, ordinary material like tissue could remind him of a snowscape, Yoshioka attempted to create a new scenery through the installation that would evoke emotions and remembrance.

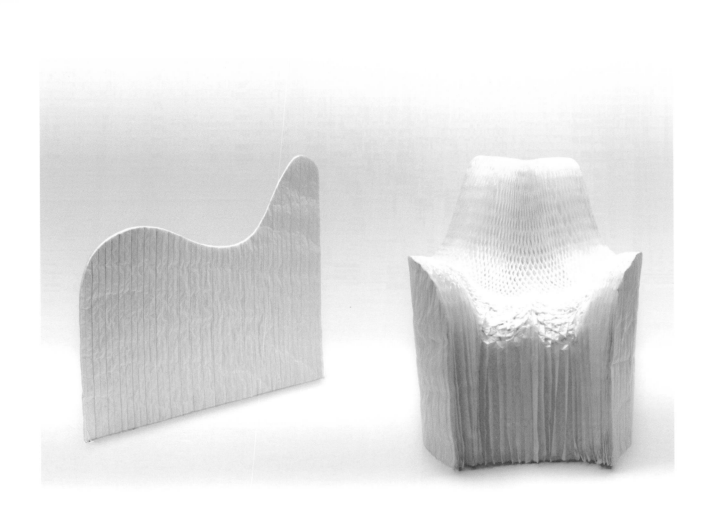

Moroso New York
2007
An installation of tissue

NENDO/AKIHIRO ITO

The cabbage chair concept was first designed by Nendo for the 'XXIst Century Man' exhibition, curated by Issey Miyake to commemorate the first anniversary of 21_21 Design Sight in Roppongi, Tokyo. Miyake asked Nendo to make furniture out of the excess pleated paper that is produced during the process of making pleated fabric. Usually abandoned as an unwanted by-product, Nendo, under the leadership of Akihiro Hito, transformed a roll of pleated paper into a small chair that appears naturally as the outside layers are peeled away, one layer at a time.

Resins added during the original paper production process add strength and the ability to remember forms, and the pleats themselves give the chair elasticity and a springy resilience. The overall effect is almost rough, but gives the user a soft, comfortable seating experience.

Since the production process is so simple, the chair has potential to be shipped as one compact roll for the user to cut open and peel back at home. There is no internal structure to the chair; it is not finished, and it is assembled without nails or screws. This primitive design responds to fabrication and distribution costs and environmental concerns, appealing to the kind of people who, to borrow a concept Miyake expressed, "don't just wear clothes, but shed their skin".

Cabbage Chair
Tokyo
2008
21_21 DESIGN SIGHT
Photo: Masayuki Hayashi

PAPER

STUDIO JOB

Designed by Studio Job for Dutch brand Mooi,
'Paper Collection' is a full range of furniture made
from paper, cardboard and papier-mâché. Each
constructed around a preliminary honeycomb mesh,
the furnishings include a cupboard, cabinet, table,
floor, lamp, pendant lights and a functional wardrobe.

Echoing childhood memories and first experiences
of making things, the designs take their lead from
classic icons but are manufactured in the manner
of modern-day furniture. The resulting products
both reflect classical style and a very contemporary
approach to material. The paper conveys to the
collection a feel that is both monumental and light,
transitory and timeless.

Chandelier
2005
Studio Job for Mooi
Wooden base, paper and cardboard

Table, Wardrobe, Chandelier
2005
Installation
Wood, paper and cardboard

JENS PRAET

The *One Day Paper Waste Table*, manufactured and distributed by Droog Design and launched at Droog Design's exhibition during the Salone del Mobile 2008, was a development of a previous limited edition series 'EatDrinkDesign' shown during Dutch Design Week in 2007. Shredded confidential documents are mixed with resin and compressed into a strong mould. The end result is a striking piece of furniture that is made with paper but has the strength of wood.

Shredded Paper Storage, constructed in a similar fashion, was commissioned by *L'Uomo Vogue* in collaboration with Yamamay, one of Italian's leading underwear brands.

Jens Praet was born in 1984 in Genk, Belgium, though now he works in Florence, Italy. He has recently opened a new studio near Florence, where he is working on a variety of projects that build on his passion for everyday objects and materials, and the combination of old and new. His inspiration draws from unexpected details and daily events, which often represent the starting-point in his designs.

One Day Paper Waste Table
2007: Manufactured by Jens Praet in an edition of 12
2008: Manufactured and distributed by Droog Design
Shredded confidential documents, resin, hardened glass plate
70 x 85 x 40 cm

PAPER

Shredded Paper Storage
2008
Shredded confidential documents, black resin
145 x 60 x 40 cm
Manufactured by Jens Praet

RESOURCES

BIBLIOGRAPHY

BOOKS:

PAPER FOLDING

Beech, Rick, *Origami, The Complete Guide to the Art of Paperfolding* (Lorenz 2001)
Engel, Peter, *Origami, from Angelfish to Zen* (Dover Press 1994)
Fukumoto, Jodi, *The Guide to American Money Folds* (Island Heritage 2004)
Fuse, Tomoko, *Fabulous Origami Boxes* (Japan Publications Trading 1998)
Fuse, Tomoko, *Kusudama Origami* (Japan Publications Trading 2002)
Gjerde, Eric, *Origami Tessellations: Awe-Inspiring Geometric Designs* (AK Peters 2008)
Hwang, Joyce, *Kirigami 1–8* (Heian 2008)
Jackson, Paul, *The Pop-up Book* (Holt Paperbacks 1994)
Kasahara, Kunihiko, *Origami Made Easy* (Japan Trading Publications 1999)
Kenneway, Eric, *Complete Origami* (St. Martin's Griffin 1987)
LaFosse, Richard, *Origami Art: Exquisite Paper Designs* (Tuttle 2008)
Lang, Robert J, *Origami Design Secrets, Mathematical Methods for an Ancient Art* (AK Peters 2003)
Mukerji, Meenakshi, *Marvelous Modular Origami* (AK Peters 2007)
Montroll, John, *Origami Sculptures* (Dover Press 1991)
Kasahara, Kunihiko, and Toshie Takahama, *Origami for the Connoisseur*
Sakai, Masako, and Michie Sahara, *Origami: Rokoan Style* (Heian International 2008)
Yamaguchi, Makoto, Kusudama: *Ball Origami* (Japan Trading Publications 1990)

PAPER CUTTING

Chinese Cut-Paper Animal Designs (Dover Press 2006)
Borja, Corinne, *Making Chinese Paper Cuts* (Albert Whitman & Co 1980)
Feng, Diane, *Chinese Paper Cutting* (Kangaroo Press 1996)
Flocken, Kathryn K, *Silhouettes: Rediscovering the Lost Art* (Paperportraits 2000)
Hahn, Angelica, *The Craft of Paper Cutting* (Search Press 1997)
Hopf, Claudia, *Papercutting: Tips, Tools and Techniques for Learning the Craft* (Stackpole 2007)
Hornung, Clarence, *Traditional Japanese Stencil Designs* (Dover 1985)
Rich, Chris, *The Book of Paper Cutting: A Complete Guide to all the Techniques* (Sterling 1994)
Shadur, Joseph, *Traditional Jewish Paper Cuts: An Inner World of Art and Symbol* (UPNE 2002)
Wagner Brust, Beth, *The Amazing Paper Cuttings of Hans Christian Andersen* (Sandpiper 2003)
Walton, Stewart, *Craft Workshop: Paper Cutting* (Southwater 2005)

PAPER ART / ARTISTS

Art on Paper magazine (New York)
Perfect Paper (Page One 2009)
The Paper Sculpture Show (exh. cat., travelling exhibition, DAP 2003)
Garrido, Maria, Ingrid Siliakus, and Joyce Aysta, *Architectural Origami: Create Models of the World's Great Buildings* (Apple 2009)
Glaubinger, Jane, *Paper Now: Bent, Molded and Manipulated* (Cleveland Museum of Art 1986)
Linssen, Nel, *Paper Jewellery* (Nel Linssen 2002)
Stephenson, Keith, and Mark Hampshire, Choosing and Using Paper for Great Graphic Design (Rotovision 2007)
Thomas, Jane, and Paul Jackson, *On Paper: New Paper Art* (Merrell 2001)
Williams, Nancy, *Paperwork* (Phaidon 1993)
Williams, Nancy, *More Paperwork* (Phaidon 2005)

WEBSITES:

www.paperstudio.com
www.artonpaper.com
www.artpaperwork.com
www.origamishrine.com
www.polyscene.com
www.origami.as
www.origami.com
www.artonpaper.com
www.artpaper.com
www.grahamhay.com.au/paper.html
www.helenmusselwhite.com
www.foldingtrees.com
www.paperforest.blogspot.com
www.thefashionspot.com/forums/f81/made-paper-62015.html
www.elsita.typepad.com/allaboutpapercutting
www.vam.ac.uk/collections/contemporary/bloodonpaper/index.html
www.iapma.info

GLOSSARY OF PAPER TERMS

Abaca/Manilla hemp
One of the earliest types of plant from which fibres are extracted to create paper.

Acid-free
Made without acidic chemicals, these papers avoid the ageing process by fending off the yellowing effects of acid.

All-rag
Paper made from rag pulp, a favourite of the Middle Ages. Today it also refers to pulp made from cotton linters.

Antique
A rough printing paper which nevertheless has a good printing surface, suitable for book printing because of its bulk.

Archival
Acid, lignin and sulphur-free paper designed specifically to keep the ageing process at bay over a long period of time.

Artists' original
High-quality imitation handmade paper, actually produced in a cylinder mould.

Blade coating
The process of levelling china clay when applied to base paper during papermaking.

Bleached mechanical
Cheaper, mechanical pulp, chemically-bleached; sometimes known as 'improved newsprint'. See also 'mechanical pulp'.

Blind embossing
A design raised from paper without ink applied.

Body stock
Paper that has not yet been coated.

Book board
Board used for the outside of hardcover books.

Broke
Paper damaged during the manufacturing process.

Calcium/magnesium carbonate buffering
The addition of calcium and magnesium carbonate to balance the natural acidity or alkalinity of a pulp.

Caliper
The thickness of a sheet of paper, usually measured in millimetres or microns.

Cartridge
Bulky, opaque paper regularly used as drawing paper.

Chemical pulp
Pulp generated through a chemical process which breaks down the fibres. Stronger and more pure than mechanical pulp, it is also less affected by light. Also known, somewhat confusingly, as 'woodfree'.

Coating
The process of coating a paper in order to enhance potential print quality. China clay coating uses a white clay.

Conditioning
Maintaining paper in optimum environmental moisture levels.

Cotton fibre
The white material found on cotton plants, the short fibres of which can be used in paper pulps.

Cylinder mould
The most common modern-day papermaking mould.

Deckle
The frame traditionally used to hold pulp in place on a mould as water is drained off.

Die-cut
The process of cutting shapes from paper using a die template.

Dimensional stability
The measure of change in the size of paper according to and as a result of environmental moisture.

Dry pressing
The pressing process applied to paper after drying.

Emulsion
Light-sensitive coating added to paper to enhance its surface.

Elemental Chlorine Free
Pulps made without the use of chlorine gas.

Filler
Substances added to paper pulps to fill in gaps in the fibre and make a surface with less see-through.

Foolscap
A common paper size, the origins of which go back to the use of 'fools' cap' watermarks in certain sizes of paper.

Formation
The distribution of fibres in a sheet of paper.

Foxing
Brown marks usually found on books suffering the effects of old age.

Glassine
A highly translucent paper.

Gloss
Usually enhanced by a coating, the gloss quality of a paper is a measure of the light-reflective level of its surface.

Grain
The direction of fibres in a sheet of paper as a result of the use of water in the process of manufacture. The fibre direction affects the stiffness of the paper when bent against or with the grain.

Grammage (gsm)
The weight of a sheet of paper, given in gsm (grams per square metre).

India
Extremely thin, high-quality and expensive paper often used for bibles.

ISO sizes
Common, international paper sizes arranged in A, B and C categories, the most famous being A4.

Ivory
A type of board commonly used for cards and menus.

Kirigami
A variant of the Japanese art of paper folding, where cutting is also deployed.

Laid
Paper formed on a laid mould. This gives it its distinctive characteristic—gentle, parallel indentations across the page.

Lens tissue
A very light tissue with high tensile strength—useful for protecting lenses, hence the name.

Loading
The process of adding minerals to paper pulp, such as China clay, to add bulk, alter opacity, or enhance colour.

Machine coating
A coating applied to base paper while on a papermaking machine.

Mechanical wood pulp
A weaker pulp ground from wood using a mechanical system, as opposed to the use of chemicals. Used for cheap newspapers and paper for novels.

Moisture content
Moisture expressed as a percentage of a paper's weight.

Mould
The wooden frame with laid or woven surface for hand-making paper.

Mould made
Imitation handmade paper made in a cylinder-mould machine.

Octavo
A paper sheet folded into eight equal-sized leaves, known as a 'section'.

Opacity
The amount of 'show-through' that a certain paper allows.

Origami
The traditional Japanese art of paper folding.

Parchment
A predecessor to paper, made from beaten sheepskin or goatskin, and favoured over paper in the West for centuries.

PH
The acidity or alkalinity of a paper, which has a bearing on its subsequent colouration over time.

Plate paper
Paper designed for copperplate printing.

Pulp
The main ingredient in the papermaking process, consisting of a variety of ingredients including cotton, rag and wood.

Satin/Silk/Matt
The most common types of paper finish, on a sliding scale of glossiness.

Simulator paper
A translucent paper known more commonly as tracing paper.

Vellum
Originally an alternative to paper made from calfskin, it now tends to exist in an imitation form.

Virgin
Paper made from fibres never previously used and selected precisely for that purpose.

Washi
The elixir of Japanese papers, often used for origami.

Black Dog Publishing Limited, London, UK, is an environmentally responsible company.

Paper is printed by Melita Press, Malta on an FSC certified paper.

Edited by Paul Sloman at Black Dog Publishing.

Designed by Matthew Pull at Black Dog Publishing.

Cover by Josh Baker and Helen Macintyre, photographed by Matthew Pull.

Design assistance by Sophie Petter and Sarah Backhouse.

Black Dog Publishing Limited

10a Acton Street

London WC1X 9NG

United Kingdom

Tel: +44 (0)20 7713 5097

Fax: +44 (0)20 7713 8682

info@blackdogonline.com

www.blackdogonline.com

ISBN 978 1 906155 58 2

British Library Cataloguing-in-Publication Data.

A CIP record for this book is available from the British Library.

architecture art design
fashion history photography
theory and things

www.blackdogonline.com

black dog
publishing

london uk